Pizza Artistry: The Canvas of Flavor

S.R. Moore

Published by S.R. Moore, 2023.

While every precaution has been taken in the preparation of this book, the publisher assumes no responsibility for errors or omissions, or for damages resulting from the use of the information contained herein.

PIZZA ARTISTRY: THE CANVAS OF FLAVOR

First edition. October 24, 2023.

ISBN: 979-8224977208

Written by S.R. Moore.

Also by S.R. Moore

Mysteries of Lavender Lane
The Secret of Lavender Lane
The Book Club Conspiracy
The Mosaic Murders

Standalone
Pizza Artistry: The Canvas of Flavor
Brews & Bites: A Beer Cheese Revolution
Souper Fusion: A Globetrotter's Culinary Journey in a Bowl
Slices of Heaven: Sandwiches Redefined for the Modern Foodie
Advent Cookies Around the World: A Global Gastronomic
Journey
Pasta for the Senses
Shamrock & Spoon: Modern Irish Cooking for Every Occasion
Autumn Harvest: Cozy Recipes for Crisp Days
The Autumn Artisan: A Global Exploration of Comfort, Craft, and
Flavor
Love in the Lavender Fields

Table of Contents

Introduction: The Art of Pizza

Pizza is more than just food—it's an edible canvas, a perfect harmony of flavors, textures, and creativity. A well-made pizza has the power to comfort, inspire, and bring people together, whether it's shared around a dinner table, at a backyard gathering, or straight from the oven on a quiet night at home. It's a dish that transcends cultures, blending tradition with innovation, simplicity with complexity.

That's what this cookbook is all about: Pizza as Art.

This book is for the home cooks, the food lovers, and the flavor adventurers. It's for those who see pizza as more than just a combination of dough, sauce, and cheese—it's a medium for culinary creativity, a way to travel the world through flavors, and a chance to break the rules of tradition while still respecting its roots. From classic artisan techniques to bold, unexpected fusions, this collection is designed to help you see pizza in a whole new way.

A Journey Through Dough & Imagination

My love for pizza started like it does for most people—with a slice. But it wasn't until I started experimenting in my own kitchen that I realized just how limitless pizza could be. The first time I stretched out dough by hand, I marveled at how something so simple—flour, water, yeast—could transform into something magical with a little patience and care. I started playing with sauces, testing different cheeses, and layering toppings in unexpected ways.

Then came the moment that changed everything: I realized that pizza could be a gateway to global flavors. Why stop at the classics when every culture has its own unique ingredients and traditions that could be woven into this familiar dish? A creamy butter chicken sauce on naan dough, smoky Korean bulgogi beef atop melted mozzarella, the bright acidity of chimichurri paired with spicy

Argentine chorizo—suddenly, pizza became more than just a dish. It became a way to tell stories, to honor traditions, and to create something entirely new.

That realization became the foundation of *Pizza Artistry: The Canvas of Flavor.*

What You'll Find in This Book

This cookbook is divided into six carefully curated sections, each one celebrating a different aspect of pizza-making:

1. **Artisan Bites & Starters** – Small bites and appetizers inspired by pizza flavors, perfect for entertaining or snacking.

2. **Inspired Accompaniments** – Side dishes that pair beautifully with pizza, featuring fresh, bold flavors.

3. **Signature Pizzas** – The heart of the book, featuring classic and inventive pizzas that elevate the art of pizza-making.

4. **Global Fusion Pizzas** – A culinary journey through different cultures, bringing international flavors into a familiar format.

5. **World Comfort Pizzas** – A collection of pizzas inspired by beloved comfort foods from around the world.

6. **Sweet Creations** – Dessert pizzas that transform simple ingredients into indulgent masterpieces.

Each section is designed to inspire, to spark curiosity, and to encourage you to step outside of your comfort zone. Whether you're looking for a familiar classic or an unexpected fusion, you'll find something in these pages that excites you.

Pizza as a Creative Expression

Cooking should never feel like a rigid set of rules—it should be a creative experience, a chance to experiment and personalize every dish to your taste. That's why this book isn't just a collection of recipes; it's an invitation to play with flavors.

Want to swap out one cheese for another? Go for it. Feel like adding an extra drizzle of something unexpected? Try it out. The beauty of pizza is that it welcomes adaptation. Some of the best recipes in this book were born out of happy accidents, last-minute substitutions, or a simple craving for something different.

Use these recipes as a starting point, a guideline—but never a limit. Let them inspire you to create, to blend flavors, and to make each pizza uniquely yours.

Your Pizza Journey Starts Here

Whether you're a seasoned home cook or someone just beginning to explore the world of homemade pizza, this book will guide you through the process. Along the way, you'll learn tips for perfecting your dough, tricks for achieving a beautifully crisp crust, and techniques for layering flavors like a pro.

So grab your favorite ingredients, fire up your oven, and get ready to turn your kitchen into a pizzeria unlike any other.

Your pizza adventure starts now—let's create something delicious.

How to Use This Cookbook

Pizza is one of the most versatile dishes in the world, and this cookbook is designed to help you create, explore, and experiment with flavors in a way that suits your personal taste. Whether you're here to master classic techniques, explore global flavors, or craft your own unique combinations, *Pizza Artistry* is built to guide you through every step of the journey.

This book is divided into six sections, each offering a different approach to pizza-making—from appetizers and sides to indulgent comfort pizzas and sweet creations. You'll find helpful tips, ingredient swaps, pairing suggestions, and customization ideas to help you make each recipe your own.

Use this cookbook however it fits your cooking style—whether that means following a recipe to the letter or using it as a foundation to inspire new creations. There are no limits when it comes to pizza!

Exploring the Six Categories

Each section of this cookbook serves a unique purpose, allowing you to create a cohesive meal or mix-and-match flavors to craft your own pizza experience.

1. Artisan Bites & Starters

Perfect for appetizers, small plates, or party snacks, this section features savory and elegant small bites that highlight pizza-inspired flavors. From crispy palmiers to stuffed tomato roses, these dishes work well as starters before diving into a full meal or as bite-sized indulgences on their own.

✔ **Best for:** Entertaining, snacking, and pairing with drinks.

✔ **Pair with:** Light salads, charcuterie boards, or sparkling beverages.

2. Inspired Accompaniments

Side dishes that complement your pizza or stand alone as flavorful additions to any meal. You'll find vibrant salads, roasted vegetables, and crispy breads that enhance the flavors of artisan pizzas.

✔ **Best for:** Rounding out a full meal with fresh and bold flavors.

✔ **Pair with:** Signature Pizzas or Fusion Pizzas to create a complete dinner.

3. Signature Pizzas

This section is the heart of the book, featuring handcrafted pizzas that showcase bold toppings, rich sauces, and perfectly balanced flavors. These pizzas range from traditional favorites to new, creative combinations designed to elevate homemade pizza to the next level.

✔ **Best for:** Mastering essential pizza-making techniques.

✔ **Pair with:** Classic side salads, light appetizers, and a crisp glass of wine or beer.

4. Global Fusion Pizzas

A culinary adventure that takes you around the world—without ever leaving your kitchen. This section introduces international flavors to the pizza format, incorporating spices, sauces, and ingredients from different cultures. You'll find Thai Peanut Chicken Pizza, Indian Butter Chicken Pizza, and Moroccan Vegetable Tagine Pizza, among others.

✔ **Best for:** Experimenting with bold, unique flavor profiles.

✔ **Pair with:** Complementary beverages (e.g., Thai iced tea, sangria, sake) for a full cultural experience.

5. World Comfort Pizzas

Comfort food meets pizza in this cozy, nostalgic collection inspired by well-loved dishes from around the world. This section includes German Pretzel & Beer Cheese Pizza, Southern BBQ Mac & Cheese Pizza, and Canadian Poutine Pizza, blending classic comfort flavors with the crispy, cheesy perfection of pizza.

✔ **Best for:** Indulgent meals, casual gatherings, and cozy nights in.

✔ **Pair with:** Warm sides like garlic knots, coleslaw, or thick-cut fries.

6. Sweet Creations

Pizza isn't just savory—this section transforms classic desserts into irresistible sweet pizzas with ingredients like fruit compotes, chocolate ganache, and caramelized toppings. Whether you're looking for a show-stopping dessert or a simple treat, these recipes bring creativity and sweetness to the pizza format.

✔ **Best for:** Dessert lovers and experimenting with unique flavor pairings.

✔ **Pair with:** Espresso, dessert wines, or a scoop of ice cream on the side.

Icons & Labels

To make it easy to navigate the recipes, you'll notice icons and labels indicating special dietary considerations and flavor profiles throughout the book. Here's what to look for:

◈ **Vegan-Friendly** – No animal products included or easily adaptable with substitutions.

◈ **Gluten-Free Option** – A gluten-free variation or adaptable with an alternative crust.

◈ **Spicy** – Recipes with bold heat levels, including gochujang, chili flakes, or spicy sauces.

◈ **Kid-Friendly** – Family-friendly recipes that are fun, simple, and loved by all ages.

◇ **Quick & Easy** – Recipes that require minimal prep time and are perfect for busy days.

Pairing Your Pizzas with Sides & Drinks

Pizza is the ultimate customizable meal, and pairing the right side dish or drink can enhance its flavors and elevate the experience. Here are some recommended pairings:

Light Pizzas (Caprese, Veggie, Mediterranean, etc.) → Pair with: Crisp salads, citrusy white wines, or sparkling lemonade.

Rich & Cheesy Pizzas (Carbonara, Mac & Cheese, Poutine, etc.) → Pair with: Garlic bread, a hoppy IPA, or a light citrusy beer.

Spicy Pizzas (Korean BBQ, Jerk Shrimp, Kimchi & Spam, etc.) → Pair with: Sweet cocktails, a cold lager, or mango lassi.

Fusion Pizzas (Thai Peanut Chicken, Moroccan Vegetable Tagine, etc.) → Pair with: Teas, sangria, or a floral white wine.

Sweet Pizzas (Chocolate Calzone, Fruit Pizza, etc.) → Pair with: Espresso, dessert wine, or vanilla gelato.

If you're preparing a full meal, mix and match pizzas with sides from different sections for a well-rounded dining experience.

- **For an Italian-inspired night:** Try a Signature Pizza with a fresh side salad and a glass of Chianti.
- **For a fun fusion dinner:** Combine a Global Fusion Pizza with Inspired Accompaniments that complement its flavors.
- **For a comfort food feast:** Pair a World Comfort Pizza with crispy fries or mac & cheese bites for indulgence.
- **For a dessert finale:** End the meal with a Sweet Creation and an espresso or dessert cocktail.

Make It Your Own

Every recipe in this book is a foundation, not a rulebook. Cooking is about creativity, exploration, and adapting recipes to your personal preferences. Here are a few ways to make these recipes your own:

◇ **Switch Up the Dough** – Try different crusts, from classic Neapolitan to thin and crispy or deep dish.

◇ **Experiment with Sauces** – Swap out traditional tomato sauce for pesto, garlic cream, or harissa-spiced bases.

◇ **Customize Toppings** – Adjust ingredients to suit your tastes, adding extra heat, sweetness, or umami flavors.

◇ **Play with Cheese Combinations** – Mix and match cheeses like smoked gouda, burrata, or blue cheese to elevate flavors.

◇ **Balance Textures** – Add crunchy nuts, crispy fried shallots, or fresh herbs for extra depth.

Whether you're a beginner or an experienced cook, this book is designed to help you craft incredible pizzas—ones that fit your taste, tell a story, and maybe even introduce you to new flavors you'll fall in love with.

So preheat your oven, gather your favorite ingredients, and get ready to turn your kitchen into an artisan pizzeria.

Essential Ingredients & Tools

Crafting the perfect pizza starts with high-quality ingredients and the right tools. Whether you're making a classic Margherita, a globally inspired fusion pizza, or an indulgent comfort creation, having a well-stocked kitchen will set you up for success. This section will guide you through the essential ingredients and equipment needed to make artisanal, restaurant-quality pizzas at home.

Essential Ingredients

The beauty of pizza is its simplicity, but the best pizzas come from fresh, high-quality ingredients. Below is a breakdown of the key ingredients that will take your pizza from good to unforgettable.

Flour & Dough Ingredients

The foundation of every great pizza is the crust, and choosing the right flour can make all the difference.

✔ **00 Flour** – Ultra-fine Italian flour that creates an airy, chewy Neapolitan-style crust. Best for high-temperature baking.

✔ **Bread Flour** – Higher protein content gives the dough a chewy texture with a slightly crisp crust.

✔ **All-Purpose Flour** – A more accessible option that works well for classic New York-style and pan pizzas.

✔ **Semolina Flour** – Often used to dust pizza peels and baking surfaces to prevent sticking and add a slight crunch.

✔ **Yeast** – Active dry yeast or instant yeast helps the dough rise and develop flavor.

✔ **Olive Oil** – Adds richness to dough and sauces while enhancing the crispiness of the crust.

✔ **Salt & Sugar** – Salt strengthens gluten in the dough, while sugar helps with browning and adds subtle sweetness.

Sauces & Base Flavors

Every pizza starts with a sauce or flavorful base—from traditional tomato to global-inspired creations.

✔ **San Marzano Tomatoes** – The gold standard for making rich, sweet tomato sauce with a perfect balance of acidity.

✔ **Tomato Paste** – Used for thicker, more concentrated sauce bases.

✔ **Garlic & Shallots** – Adds depth and richness to sauces and flavored oils.

✔ **Balsamic Vinegar** – Enhances tomato-based sauces and works beautifully as a finishing drizzle.

✔ **Pesto (Basil or Sun-Dried Tomato)** – A bold, herby alternative to tomato sauce.

✔ **Garlic-Infused Olive Oil** – A flavorful alternative to traditional sauce, often used in white pizzas.

◇ **Global Sauce Staples**

✔ **Gochujang (Korea)** – A fermented chili paste that adds depth, sweetness, and heat to fusion pizzas.

✔ **Harissa (North Africa)** – A smoky, spicy pepper paste perfect for bold, layered flavors.

✔ **Chimichurri (Argentina)** – A herby, garlicky sauce that adds brightness and contrast.

✔ **Tzatziki (Greece)** – A cooling yogurt-based sauce ideal for Mediterranean pizzas.

✔ **Peanut Sauce (Thailand)** – A rich, slightly sweet base that pairs well with chicken or shrimp.

Cheese Selection

Pizza wouldn't be pizza without melted, gooey cheese, but not all cheeses are created equal.

✔ **Mozzarella (Low-Moisture)** – The classic stretchy, melty cheese used for most pizzas.

✔ **Fresh Mozzarella** – Best for Neapolitan-style pizzas, with creamy flavor and excellent melt.

✔ **Parmesan & Pecorino Romano** – Adds a salty, nutty finish when grated over hot pizza.

✔ **Ricotta** – Light and creamy, perfect for white pizzas or dolloping on top.

✔ **Goat Cheese & Feta** – Tangy and slightly crumbly, these cheeses pair well with Mediterranean flavors.

✔ **Smoked Gouda** – A great addition to BBQ pizzas for extra smokiness.

✔ **Blue Cheese & Gorgonzola** – Bold, funky cheeses that work well with sweet ingredients like honey or figs.

Toppings & Garnishes

The best pizzas balance flavor, texture, and color. Here are must-have toppings that will bring your pizzas to life.

✔ **Fresh Herbs (Basil, Oregano, Thyme, Cilantro, Mint, Parsley)** – Adds bright, aromatic notes.

✔ **Red Onion & Shallots** – Slightly sweet when caramelized, perfect for savory pizzas.

✔ **Roasted Garlic** – Deep, rich flavor that elevates white pizzas and tomato-based pies.

✔ **Mushrooms (Cremini, Portobello, Shiitake, Enoki)** – Adds umami and depth.

✔ **Cured Meats (Prosciutto, Salami, Soppressata, Chorizo)** – Adds saltiness and richness.

✔ **Marinated Olives & Capers** – Briny, salty elements that bring balance.

✔ **Eggs** – Used in carbonara-style pizzas or baked directly on top.

✔ **Fresh Greens (Arugula, Spinach, Microgreens)** – Adds a peppery bite after baking.

◈ **Global Topping Inspirations**

✔ **Kimchi (Korea)** – Fermented, spicy cabbage that adds depth to fusion pizzas.

✔ **Preserved Lemons (Morocco)** – Intense citrusy brightness.

✔ **Pineapple & Mango (Hawaii & Caribbean)** – Sweet acidity for tropical flavors.

✔ **Jalapeños & Scotch Bonnet Peppers (Mexico & Caribbean)** – For those who love heat.

✔ **Tandoori Chicken (India)** – A rich, spiced protein that pairs well with creamy sauces.

Essential Tools

Equipping your kitchen with the right tools will help you achieve crispier crusts, even cooking, and a professional-quality pizza experience.

Baking & Cooking Equipment

✔ **Pizza Stone or Baking Steel** – Retains heat and mimics a wood-fired oven, creating a perfectly crispy crust.

✔ **Pizza Peel** – Essential for transferring pizzas in and out of the oven without tearing the dough.

✔ **Rolling Pin** – Helps evenly shape dough, especially for thin-crust styles.

✔ **Bench Scraper** – Makes handling sticky dough easier.

✔ **Cooling Rack** – Prevents pizzas from getting soggy by allowing air circulation under the crust.

Cutting & Serving Tools

✔ **Sharp Chef's Knife or Pizza Cutter** – A must-have for clean, even slices.

✔ **Herb Scissors** – Perfect for fresh basil, cilantro, or parsley toppings.

✔ **Cheese Grater & Microplane** – Ideal for grating fresh Parmesan or zesting citrus.

Dough Preparation

✔ **Proofing Containers or Large Mixing Bowls** – Helps ferment dough properly and develop flavor.

✔ **Digital Kitchen Scale** – Essential for measuring flour and ingredients for consistent dough.

✔ **Instant-Read Thermometer** – Ensures the dough is at the correct temperature for baking.

Stocking Your Kitchen for Pizza Success

To set yourself up for success, here are a few quick tips:

◇ **Keep staple ingredients stocked** – Flour, yeast, olive oil, and canned tomatoes should always be on hand.

◇ **Experiment with new ingredients** – Try a new cheese, sauce, or spice blend each time you make a pizza.

◇ **Invest in a good pizza stone** – It's one of the easiest ways to elevate your homemade pizza.

◇ **Use high-quality cheeses and fresh toppings** – Better ingredients = better pizza.

With these essential ingredients and tools, you're ready to craft pizzeria-quality pizzas from the comfort of your own kitchen. Whether you're going for classic simplicity or bold, fusion-inspired creations, these elements will help you achieve the perfect pizza every time. ◇◇

Dough & Sauce Guide

Great pizza starts with a solid foundation—the dough and the sauce. These two elements set the tone for the entire pizza, determining its texture, flavor, and how well it holds up to toppings. Whether you love a thin, crispy crust, a pillowy Neapolitan-style pizza, or a deep-dish indulgence, this section will guide you through different dough options and flavorful sauce variations to help you craft the perfect base for your creations.

This guide includes:

✔ **Classic Pizza Dough (All-Purpose)** – A versatile dough perfect for most pizzas.

✔ **Neapolitan-Style Dough** – Light, airy, and crispy, designed for high-heat baking.

✔ **Thin & Crispy Dough** – For those who love a cracker-like crust.

✔ **Deep-Dish Dough** – Buttery and rich, perfect for layered, indulgent pizzas.

✔ **Gluten-Free Dough** – A delicious alternative for gluten-sensitive pizza lovers.

✔ **Essential Sauces** – Classic tomato, white garlic cream, pesto, and globally inspired bases.

Essential Dough Recipes

1. Classic Pizza Dough (All-Purpose)

A balanced, chewy crust that works well for everything from classic Margherita to loaded supreme pizzas.

Ingredients

- 3 ½ cups (440g) all-purpose or bread flour
- 1 teaspoon salt
- 1 packet (2 ¼ teaspoons) active dry yeast or instant yeast
- 1 ¼ cups (300ml) warm water (110°F or 43°C)

- 1 tablespoon olive oil
- 1 teaspoon sugar (optional, for extra browning)

Instructions

1. **Activate the Yeast**: In a small bowl, combine warm water, sugar, and yeast. Let sit for 5-10 minutes until foamy.
2. **Mix the Dough**: In a large bowl, combine flour and salt. Slowly add the yeast mixture and olive oil. Mix until a shaggy dough forms.
3. **Knead**: Transfer to a floured surface and knead for 8-10 minutes until smooth and elastic.
4. **First Rise**: Place in a greased bowl, cover with a damp cloth, and let rise for 1-2 hours or until doubled in size.
5. **Shape & Bake**: Punch down the dough, roll out to your preferred thickness, and bake at 500°F (260°C) for 7-10 minutes or until golden and crisp.

✔ **Best for:** New York-style pizza, classic cheese, and most traditional toppings.

✔ **Pro Tip:** For extra flavor, let the dough cold ferment in the fridge for 24-48 hours.

---

2. Neapolitan-Style Dough

This traditional Italian dough has an airy, bubbly crust and crisps beautifully in high heat.

Ingredients

- 4 cups (500g) 00 flour (Italian-style fine flour)
- 1 ½ teaspoons salt
- 1 packet (2 ¼ teaspoons) instant yeast
- 1 ¼ cups (300ml) cold water
- 1 tablespoon olive oil

Instructions

1. In a large bowl, combine flour and salt.
2. Dissolve yeast in cold water, then mix into the flour. Stir until a sticky dough forms.
3. Knead the dough for 8-10 minutes until smooth.
4. Cover and let rise for 8-24 hours at room temperature for best results.
5. Punch down, shape into balls, and roll into a thin, circular shape.
6. Bake at 800°F (425°C) in a pizza oven or on a preheated stone at 500°F (260°C) for 60-90 seconds.

✔ **Best for:** Classic Margherita, Caprese, and light toppings.

✔ **Pro Tip:** Neapolitan dough requires high heat—a pizza stone or baking steel is highly recommended!

3. Thin & Crispy Dough

A light, cracker-like crust with extra crispness.

Ingredients

- 2 cups (250g) all-purpose flour
- 1 teaspoon salt
- 1 teaspoon baking powder (for extra crispiness)
- ½ cup (120ml) warm water
- 2 tablespoons olive oil

Instructions

1. Mix dry ingredients, then gradually add water and olive oil.
2. Knead for only 2-3 minutes until smooth.
3. Roll out very thin (⅛-inch or thinner) for a super crispy crust.
4. Bake at 450°F (230°C) for 8-10 minutes until golden.

✔ **Best for:** Pesto, BBQ chicken, or veggie-loaded pizzas.

✔ **Pro Tip:** No need for yeast! This dough is quick and easy for weeknight pizzas.

4. Deep-Dish Dough

A buttery, thick, and flaky crust for Chicago-style pizzas.

Ingredients

- 3 ¼ cups (410g) all-purpose flour
- 1 teaspoon salt
- 1 packet (2 ¼ teaspoons) instant yeast
- ½ cup (120ml) warm water
- ¼ cup (60g) melted butter
- 2 tablespoons olive oil

Instructions

1. Combine dry ingredients, then mix in water, butter, and oil.
2. Knead until smooth, then let rise for 2 hours.
3. Press into a deep-dish pan, layering cheese first, then toppings, and finally sauce.
4. Bake at 425°F (220°C) for 25-30 minutes.

✔ **Best for:** Meat-lovers, extra cheese-heavy pizzas, and hearty toppings.

✔ **Pro Tip: Butter in the dough** adds flakiness—don't skip it!

5. Gluten-Free Dough

A light, crispy crust alternative that's still delicious.

Ingredients

- 2 cups (250g) gluten-free flour blend
- 1 teaspoon salt
- 1 teaspoon xanthan gum (if not included in flour blend)
- 2 teaspoons baking powder

- 1 packet (2 ¼ teaspoons) instant yeast
- 1 cup (240ml) warm water
- 2 tablespoons olive oil

Instructions

1. Combine dry ingredients, then slowly add water and oil.
2. Mix until smooth and slightly sticky.
3. Let rest for 30-45 minutes before rolling out.
4. Bake at 425°F (220°C) for 10-12 minutes before adding toppings, then return to bake for another 5-7 minutes.

✔ **Best for:** Any toppings—holds up well!

✔ **Pro Tip:** Brush with garlic butter before baking for extra flavor.

Essential Sauce Recipes

1. Classic Tomato Sauce

- 1 can (28 oz) San Marzano tomatoes
- 2 tablespoons olive oil
- 2 cloves garlic, minced
- 1 teaspoon dried oregano
- ½ teaspoon salt
- ¼ teaspoon black pepper

◈ **Pro Tip:** Simmer for 20-30 minutes for a deeper flavor.

2. White Garlic Cream Sauce

- 2 tablespoons butter
- 2 cloves garlic, minced
- 1 cup heavy cream
- ½ cup Parmesan cheese

◈ **Pro Tip:** Add a pinch of nutmeg for warmth.

3. Spicy Harissa Sauce

- 2 tablespoons harissa paste
- ½ cup crushed tomatoes
- 1 teaspoon cumin

◈ **Pro Tip:** Great for Moroccan or Middle Eastern pizzas.

With these dough and sauce recipes, you're ready to build incredible pizzas from the ground up! Experiment, mix flavors, and create your signature style. ◈◈

Artisan Bites & Starters

1. **Mozzarella-Stuffed Tomato Roses**: Delicate tomato slices filled with fresh mozzarella, rolled into rose shapes, and drizzled with balsamic reduction.

2. **Pesto Palmiers**: Flaky puff pastry spirals filled with homemade basil pesto, parmesan, and pine nuts.

3. **Edible Flower Bruschetta**: Colorful bruschetta topped with a mix of edible flowers, heirloom tomatoes, olive oil, and a touch of balsamic glaze.

4. **Savory Ricotta-Stuffed Mini Peppers**: Roasted mini sweet peppers filled with a creamy ricotta and herb mixture.

5. **Geometric Caprese Skewers**: Cherry tomatoes, fresh mozzarella, and basil leaves arranged on skewers to form eye-catching geometric patterns, drizzled with a balsamic reduction.

6. **Asparagus and Prosciutto Bundles**: Blanched asparagus spears wrapped in thinly sliced prosciutto and served with a lemon-dill dipping sauce.

7. **Artichoke Heart Petals**: Marinated artichoke hearts arranged like flower petals and served with a garlic aioli.

8. **Mushroom Ceviche**: Sliced mushrooms marinated in lime juice, mixed with diced red onion, cilantro, and jalapeños for a zesty, non-traditional ceviche.

9. **Polenta Bites with Sundried Tomato Tapenade**: Polenta rounds grilled to perfection and topped with a flavorful sundried tomato tapenade.

10. **Cucumber Canvases**: Cucumber slices cut into artistic shapes and adorned with herbed cream cheese, smoked salmon, and capers.

Mozzarella-Stuffed Tomato Roses

Serving Size: 4 servings

Prep Time: 15 minutes

Cook Time: 15 minutes

Total Time: 30 minutes

Ingredients

- 4 large, ripe tomatoes
- 8 fresh mozzarella balls
- 1 cup balsamic vinegar
- 1-2 tablespoons honey, maple syrup, or brown sugar (optional, for added sweetness)
- Fresh basil leaves (for garnish)
- Salt and freshly ground pepper (to taste)

Instructions

1. **Prepare the Balsamic Reduction:**
   - Pour the balsamic vinegar into a small, heavy-bottomed saucepan. If you prefer a sweeter reduction, stir in honey, maple syrup, or brown sugar.
   - Place the saucepan over medium heat and bring the vinegar to a gentle simmer. Avoid boiling, as this can cause the vinegar to scorch.
   - Once simmering, reduce the heat to low and let it cook, stirring occasionally, until the liquid is reduced by about half. This should take 10-15 minutes.
   - The reduction is ready when it coats the back of a spoon and has a syrupy consistency. Remember, it

will thicken further as it cools.

- ○ Remove the pan from heat and let the reduction cool to room temperature. Set aside.

2. **Prepare the Tomatoes:**
   - ○ Slice each tomato thinly into even rounds, aiming for about 8 slices per tomato. Try to maintain consistent thickness for easy rolling.

3. **Form the Roses:**
   - ○ Lay 2-3 slices of tomato slightly overlapping in a line.
   - ○ Place a mozzarella ball on one end of the line and gently roll the tomato slices around it to create a rose shape. Secure the base with a toothpick if necessary. Repeat for all the tomato slices and mozzarella balls.

4. **Plate the Roses:**
   - ○ Arrange the tomato roses on a serving platter.
   - ○ Drizzle balsamic reduction over the roses for a touch of sweetness and tang.
   - ○ Garnish with fresh basil leaves and a sprinkle of salt and pepper.

5. **Serve:**
   - ○ Serve immediately, or chill for 15 minutes for a refreshing appetizer.

Tips for the Balsamic Reduction:

- Keep an eye on the vinegar as it reduces. It can go from perfect to overcooked quickly.
- If it thickens too much, add a splash of water and stir over low heat to loosen it.

Nutritional Information (Per Serving)

- Calories: 150
- Protein: 8g
- Fat: 10g
  - Saturated Fat: 6g
- Carbohydrates: 5g
  - Fiber: 1g
  - Sugar: 3g
- Sodium: 150mg
- Cholesterol: 30mg

Mozzarella-Stuffed Tomato Roses are a product of serendipity and summer inspiration. One warm evening, I found myself with fresh tomatoes from the garden and creamy mozzarella from the farmer's market. Wanting to create something visually stunning and simple, the idea of roses struck me as I admired the tomatoes' vibrant hue. This dish quickly became a favorite at family gatherings—not just for its flavor but for the admiration it garners for its artistic presentation. Whenever I serve it, there's always a moment of awe before the first bite, and that's what makes this appetizer so special.

Feel free to customize this recipe with different cheeses, such as goat cheese or feta, or even add a layer of prosciutto for a savory twist. These edible roses are the perfect centerpiece for a table, proving that food truly is art.

Notes

- *Tomato Selection*: Opt for tomatoes that are firm but ripe to ensure they hold their shape while rolling. Heirloom tomatoes work wonderfully for adding a variety of colors.
- *Mozzarella Variations*: Try smoked mozzarella for a subtle, smoky flavor or burrata for extra creaminess.
- *Additional Enhancements*: Wrapping the tomato roses with thin strips of prosciutto can elevate the flavor profile with a

savory element. You can also add a sprinkle of crushed nuts, like pistachios, for texture.

- *Serving Suggestions*: Pair these roses with a crusty baguette or alongside a simple arugula salad to create a complete appetizer course.

Pesto Palmiers

Serving Size: 12 servings
Prep Time: 15 minutes
Cook Time: 15-20 minutes
Total Time: 35 minutes

Ingredients
For the Palmiers:

- 1 sheet puff pastry, thawed
- 1/4 cup grated Parmesan cheese
- 2 tablespoons pine nuts

For the Basil Pesto:

- 2 cups fresh basil leaves, packed
- 1/4 cup grated Parmesan cheese
- 1/4 cup pine nuts
- 2 cloves garlic
- 1/4 cup extra virgin olive oil (plus more if needed)
- Salt and freshly ground black pepper (to taste)

Instructions
Make the Basil Pesto:

1. **Prepare the Ingredients:**
   - Wash and pat dry the basil leaves.
   - Toast the pine nuts in a dry skillet over medium heat for 2-3 minutes, shaking occasionally, until golden and fragrant.
2. **Blend the Pesto:**
   - In a food processor, combine basil leaves, Parmesan cheese, toasted pine nuts, and garlic.

Pulse until the ingredients are finely chopped.
  - With the processor running, slowly drizzle in the olive oil until the pesto reaches your desired consistency. Add more oil if necessary.
  - Season with salt and pepper to taste.

Prepare the Palmiers:

1. **Preheat the Oven:**
   - Preheat your oven to 375°F (190°C). Line a baking sheet with parchment paper.
2. **Roll Out the Puff Pastry:**
   - Lay the puff pastry sheet on a lightly floured surface. Roll it out slightly to create an even layer.
3. **Spread the Pesto:**
   - Spread an even layer of the prepared basil pesto over the entire surface of the puff pastry.
4. **Add the Toppings:**
   - Sprinkle grated Parmesan cheese and pine nuts evenly over the pesto layer.
5. **Shape the Palmiers:**
   - Roll one side of the puff pastry towards the center. Then roll the opposite side towards the center to meet the first roll, forming a double-spiral log.
   - Gently press the rolls together and wrap the log in plastic wrap. Chill in the refrigerator for 10-15 minutes to firm up.
6. **Slice and Bake:**
   - Using a sharp knife, slice the log into 1/2-inch thick pieces. Arrange the slices cut-side up on the prepared baking sheet, leaving space between each piece.
   - Bake in the preheated oven for 15-20 minutes, or

until golden brown and flaky.

7. **Serve:**
   - Allow the palmiers to cool slightly before serving. They are best enjoyed warm or at room temperature.

Nutritional Information (Per Serving)

- Calories: 120
- Protein: 3g
- Fat: 9g
  - Saturated Fat: 3g
- Carbohydrates: 9g
  - Fiber: 1g
  - Sugar: 0g
- Sodium: 75mg
- Cholesterol: 5mg

Pesto Palmiers bring together two of my favorite culinary loves: buttery puff pastry and the vibrant flavors of homemade basil pesto. The first time I made these, it was for a summer picnic with friends. I remember the look of delight as everyone reached for these golden spirals, their flaky layers revealing a swirl of green pesto and nutty Parmesan. These palmiers quickly became my go-to appetizer for any gathering. They're elegant yet simple, proving that a few quality ingredients can create a show-stopping dish.

Over the years, I've experimented with variations, adding sun-dried tomatoes or swapping pine nuts for walnuts. But the classic basil version remains my favorite. The best part? They're just as delicious the next day—if there are any leftovers! I hope this recipe becomes a cherished part of your culinary repertoire, just as it has been for me.

Notes

- *Pesto Tips*: For a twist, experiment with different pesto bases like arugula, sun-dried tomato, or spinach. Adding a hint of lemon zest to the pesto can brighten the flavor.
- *Storage and Reheating*: Store baked palmiers in an airtight container for up to 2 days. Reheat in the oven at 350°F (175°C) for 5 minutes to restore crispness.
- *Presentation*: Arrange the palmiers in a circular pattern on a platter for a visually striking presentation at parties. Pair with a dipping sauce, such as a roasted red pepper aioli or marinara, for added flavor.

Edible Flower Bruschetta

Serving Size: 12 servings
    Prep Time: 30 minutes
    Cook Time: 30 minutes
    Total Time: 1 hour

Ingredients
For the French Baguette:

- 2 1/4 teaspoons (1 packet) active dry yeast
- 1 1/2 cups warm water (110°F/45°C)
- 3 1/4 cups all-purpose flour
- 1 1/2 teaspoons salt
- 1 teaspoon sugar

For the Bruschetta:

- 1 French baguette (homemade or store-bought)
- 2 cup heirloom cherry tomatoes, halved
- 1/4 cup extra virgin olive oil
- 2 tablespoons balsamic glaze
- 1 cup edible flowers (e.g., pansies, nasturtiums, violas)
- 1/4 teaspoon sea salt
- Freshly ground black pepper (to taste)
- Fresh basil leaves (optional, for garnish)

Instructions
Make the French Baguette:

1. **Activate the Yeast:**
    - In a large mixing bowl, dissolve the sugar in warm water. Sprinkle the yeast over the top and let it sit for 5-10 minutes until frothy.

2. **Mix the Dough:**
   - Add the salt and 2 cups of flour to the yeast mixture. Stir until combined. Gradually add the remaining flour until a dough forms.
3. **Knead the Dough:**
   - Turn the dough out onto a floured surface and knead for 8-10 minutes until smooth and elastic. If the dough is sticky, add a little more flour as needed.
4. **First Rise:**
   - Place the dough in a lightly greased bowl, cover with a damp cloth, and let it rise in a warm place for 1 hour or until doubled in size.
5. **Shape the Baguette:**
   - Punch down the dough and divide it into two equal parts. Shape each into a long, thin loaf (about 12-14 inches). Place the loaves on a baking sheet lined with parchment paper.
6. **Second Rise:**
   - Cover the loaves with a damp cloth and let them rise again for 30 minutes.
7. **Bake the Baguette:**
   - Preheat your oven to 450°F (230°C). Place a shallow pan of water on the bottom rack to create steam.
   - Bake the baguettes for 20-25 minutes, or until golden brown and crusty. Allow to cool before slicing.

Prepare the Bruschetta:

1. **Slice the Baguette:**
   - Once cooled, slice the baguette into 1/2-inch

thick pieces. Lightly toast the slices under a broiler or in a toaster oven until golden brown.

2. **Prepare the Topping:**
   - In a bowl, toss the halved cherry tomatoes with olive oil, sea salt, and black pepper. Set aside.

3. **Assemble the Bruschetta:**
   - Spread the tomato mixture evenly on each toasted baguette slice.
   - Top with a scattering of edible flowers for color and flavor.
   - Drizzle balsamic glaze over the assembled bruschetta.

4. **Garnish and Serve:**
   - Garnish with fresh basil leaves if desired. Serve immediately.

Nutritional Information (Per Serving)

- Calories: 120
- Protein: 3g
- Fat: 5g
   - Saturated Fat: 1g
- Carbohydrates: 16g
   - Fiber: 1g
   - Sugar: 2g
- Sodium: 200mg
- Cholesterol: 0mg

The first time I made Edible Flower Bruschetta was for a spring garden party. The bright, colorful flowers complemented the sweet heirloom tomatoes so perfectly that it felt like serving a plate of art. Guests were hesitant at first, unsure about eating flowers, but one bite changed everything. The floral notes, combined with the tang of balsamic glaze and the crunch of freshly baked baguette, made this dish an instant favorite.

Making the baguette from scratch adds a personal touch that elevates the entire experience, but store-bought works wonderfully for a quick preparation. Each time I make this dish, it reminds me of that sunny afternoon, the laughter of friends, and the joy of creating something truly beautiful and delicious. It's a celebration of nature on a plate, perfect for any occasion.

Notes

- *Flower Selection*: Use a mix of edible flowers for flavor and color contrast. Nasturtiums provide a peppery note, while violas are mild and sweet.
- *Seasonal Variations*: Swap the tomatoes for seasonal produce like peaches or figs during summer, or roasted squash in the fall.
- *Make-Ahead Tip*: Assemble the tomato mixture a few hours ahead and store in the fridge. Add the flowers just before serving to prevent wilting.
- *Wine Pairing*: This dish pairs wonderfully with a crisp Sauvignon Blanc or a light Rosé.

Savory Ricotta-Stuffed Mini Peppers

Serving Size: 12 servings
Prep Time: 15 minutes
Cook Time: 20 minutes
Total Time: 35 minutes

Ingredients

For the Peppers:

- 12 mini sweet peppers
- 1 tablespoon olive oil
- Salt and freshly ground black pepper (to taste)

For the Ricotta Filling:

- 1 cup ricotta cheese
- 2 tablespoons grated Parmesan cheese
- 2 tablespoons fresh herbs (e.g., basil, parsley, and chives), finely chopped
- 1 teaspoon lemon zest
- 1 clove garlic, minced
- 1/4 teaspoon red pepper flakes (optional, for heat)
- Salt and freshly ground black pepper (to taste)

Optional Garnish:

- Additional fresh herbs
- Grated Parmesan cheese
- Drizzle of olive oil

Instructions

1. **Prepare the Peppers:**

- Preheat your oven to 375°F (190°C).
  - Slice the tops off the mini sweet peppers and remove the seeds and membranes. Brush the insides and outsides lightly with olive oil. Sprinkle with a pinch of salt and black pepper.

2. **Make the Ricotta Filling:**
   - In a medium bowl, combine the ricotta cheese, Parmesan cheese, fresh herbs, lemon zest, minced garlic, red pepper flakes (if using), and a pinch of salt and black pepper. Mix until smooth and well combined.

3. **Stuff the Peppers:**
   - Use a small spoon or piping bag to fill each mini pepper generously with the ricotta mixture.

4. **Roast the Peppers:**
   - Arrange the stuffed peppers upright on a baking sheet lined with parchment paper or in a small baking dish to hold them steady.
   - Roast in the preheated oven for 15-20 minutes, or until the peppers are tender and slightly charred, and the filling is lightly golden on top.

5. **Garnish and Serve:**
   - Remove the peppers from the oven and let them cool slightly. Garnish with additional fresh herbs, a sprinkle of grated Parmesan, or a drizzle of olive oil, if desired. Serve warm.

Nutritional Information (Per Serving)

- Calories: 50
- Protein: 2g
- Fat: 3g
  - Saturated Fat: 1.5g

- Carbohydrates: 3g
  - Fiber: 1g
  - Sugar: 2g
- Sodium: 70mg
- Cholesterol: 7mg

This recipe was born out of my love for vibrant, fresh flavors and my habit of always having mini sweet peppers in the fridge. It started as an experiment to elevate a simple appetizer, and it quickly became a family favorite. The creamy ricotta filling, brightened with fresh herbs and lemon zest, pairs beautifully with the natural sweetness of the roasted peppers.

One summer evening, I brought a tray of these to a neighborhood potluck, and they were gone before I even had a chance to grab one! What I love most about this dish is how versatile it is—you can swap the herbs to suit your taste, or add a touch of heat for those who like a spicy kick. These stuffed mini peppers are the perfect balance of elegance and comfort, proving that a simple recipe can create a big impact.

Notes

- *Customizations*: Experiment with different cheeses such as goat cheese or cream cheese for variation. Add diced sun-dried tomatoes, olives, or crumbled bacon to the filling for added depth.
- *Serving Idea*: These peppers can also be served cold as part of a charcuterie board. Simply chill after roasting for a refreshing twist.
- *Perfect Pairing*: Pair with a sparkling wine or Prosecco for a light, celebratory combination.

Geometric Caprese Skewers

Serving Size: 12 servings
Prep Time: 20 minutes
Cook Time: 15 minutes
Total Time: 35 minutes

Ingredients
For the Skewers:

- 24 cherry tomatoes (red and yellow for variety)
- 12 fresh mozzarella balls
- 24 fresh basil leaves
- 12 wooden or metal skewers (approximately 6 inches long)

For the Balsamic Reduction:

- 1 cup balsamic vinegar
- 1-2 tablespoons honey, maple syrup, or brown sugar (optional, for sweetness)

Optional Garnish:

- Flaky sea salt
- Freshly ground black pepper

Instructions

1. **Prepare the Balsamic Reduction (if not store-bought):**
   - In a small, heavy-bottomed saucepan, pour the balsamic vinegar.
   - If desired, add honey, maple syrup, or brown sugar to balance the tanginess.
   - Place over medium heat and bring to a gentle

simmer.

- Reduce the heat to low and let it cook, stirring occasionally, until the liquid reduces by half and becomes syrupy (approximately 10-15 minutes).
- Remove from heat and let cool to room temperature. The reduction will thicken further as it cools.

2. **Assemble the Skewers:**
   - On each skewer, thread a cherry tomato, a basil leaf, and a mozzarella ball. Repeat the pattern to fill the skewer, ensuring a visually appealing geometric arrangement. For variety, alternate the colors of tomatoes and angle the basil leaves for a layered effect.

3. **Plate the Skewers:**
   - Arrange the completed skewers on a clean white platter or tray in parallel lines or a circular pattern for a visually striking presentation.

4. **Drizzle and Garnish:**
   - Lightly drizzle the skewers with the cooled balsamic reduction.
   - Sprinkle with flaky sea salt and freshly ground black pepper for added flavor.

5. **Serve:**
   - Serve immediately as a fresh, vibrant appetizer. These skewers can also be made ahead and refrigerated for up to 2 hours. If refrigerated, drizzle the balsamic reduction just before serving to maintain its texture and sheen.

Nutritional Information (Per Serving)

- Calories: 40

- Protein: 2g
- Fat: 3g
  - Saturated Fat: 1.5g
- Carbohydrates: 2g
  - Fiber: 0g
  - Sugar: 1g
- Sodium: 40mg
- Cholesterol: 5mg

Geometric Caprese Skewers came to life while preparing appetizers for a summer garden party. I wanted something that combined the freshness of Caprese salad with a modern, artistic twist. The idea of skewers struck me as a way to make the dish portable and visually striking.

Threading the ingredients in a geometric pattern added a playful, yet elegant, touch that wowed my guests. Watching their delight as they admired—and then devoured—the skewers was a reminder of how food can be both a feast for the eyes and the palate. These skewers are my go-to for gatherings because they're easy to prepare, incredibly fresh, and always a hit. Plus, the balsamic reduction adds just the right amount of sweetness and tang to tie everything together beautifully.

Notes

- *Tomato Choices*: Use heirloom cherry tomatoes for a range of colors, enhancing the visual appeal of the skewers.
- *Creative Presentation*: Alternate skewer lengths to create a visually dynamic serving platter. Shorter skewers work well for individual servings, while longer skewers make a bold statement.
- *Balsamic Alternatives*: For a sweeter option, use a balsamic glaze infused with honey or fig.

Asparagus and Prosciutto Bundles

Serving Size: 12 servings
Prep Time: 15 minutes
Cook Time: 10 minutes
Total Time: 25 minutes

Ingredients
For the Bundles:

- 12 asparagus spears, woody ends trimmed
- 6 thin slices of prosciutto, halved lengthwise
- 1 tablespoon olive oil
- Freshly ground black pepper (to taste)

For the Lemon-Dill Dipping Sauce:

- 1/2 cup Greek yogurt
- 1 tablespoon mayonnaise (optional, for creaminess)
- 1 teaspoon lemon zest
- 1 tablespoon fresh lemon juice
- 1 tablespoon fresh dill, finely chopped
- 1/2 teaspoon garlic powder
- Salt and freshly ground black pepper (to taste)

Instructions

1. **Prepare the Asparagus:**
   - Bring a large pot of salted water to a boil.
   - Blanch the asparagus spears by boiling them for 2 minutes, then immediately transfer them to a bowl of ice water to halt the cooking process. Drain and pat dry with a clean towel.
2. **Wrap the Asparagus:**

- ◦ Take one blanched asparagus spear and wrap it tightly with a halved slice of prosciutto. Repeat for all asparagus spears.

3. **Cook the Bundles:**
   - ◦ Heat a large skillet over medium heat and add the olive oil.
   - ◦ Place the prosciutto-wrapped asparagus bundles in the skillet in a single layer. Cook for 2-3 minutes per side, turning carefully, until the prosciutto is crisp and the asparagus is tender.

4. **Make the Lemon-Dill Dipping Sauce:**
   - ◦ In a small bowl, whisk together the Greek yogurt, mayonnaise (if using), lemon zest, lemon juice, dill, garlic powder, salt, and pepper until smooth. Adjust seasoning to taste. Cover and refrigerate until ready to serve.

5. **Serve:**
   - ◦ Arrange the warm asparagus bundles on a serving plate. Serve immediately with the lemon-dill dipping sauce on the side.

Nutritional Information (Per Serving)

- Calories: 45
- Protein: 3g
- Fat: 3g
  - ◦ Saturated Fat: 1g
- Carbohydrates: 1g
  - ◦ Fiber: 0g
  - ◦ Sugar: 0g
- Sodium: 120mg
- Cholesterol: 5mg

Asparagus and Prosciutto Bundles have become a staple appetizer in my kitchen, especially for springtime gatherings. The first time I made this dish, I was hosting a small Easter brunch and wanted something elegant yet easy to prepare. The contrast between the salty, crisp prosciutto and the fresh, slightly tender asparagus was an instant hit, but it was the lemon-dill dipping sauce that really stole the show.

I remember my guests praising the lightness of the sauce, which complemented the richness of the prosciutto perfectly. This dish not only looks sophisticated but also highlights the beauty of seasonal produce. Whenever I serve these bundles, they bring back memories of lively conversations and laughter around the table, making them as special as the moments they've helped create.

Notes

- *Substitution Options*: Swap prosciutto for thinly sliced smoked salmon or turkey for a different flavor.
- *Dipping Sauce Variations*: Add a touch of horseradish or Dijon mustard to the lemon-dill sauce for extra zing.
- *Serving Idea*: These bundles are versatile and can be served warm, room temperature, or cold, making them perfect for any event.

Artichoke Heart Petals with Garlic Aioli

Serving Size: 4 servings
Prep Time: 10 minutes
Cook Time: 0 minutes
Total Time: 10 minutes

Ingredients
For the Artichoke Petals:

- 1 jar (14 oz) marinated artichoke hearts, drained and quartered
- 1 tablespoon extra virgin olive oil (optional, for extra shine)
- Fresh parsley or dill (optional, for garnish)

For the Garlic Aioli:

- 1/2 cup mayonnaise
- 1 clove garlic, finely minced or grated
- 1 teaspoon fresh lemon juice
- 1/2 teaspoon Dijon mustard
- Salt and freshly ground black pepper (to taste)

Instructions

1. **Prepare the Artichoke Petals:**
   - Drain the marinated artichoke hearts well and pat them dry with a paper towel to remove excess oil.
   - Arrange the artichoke hearts on a serving platter in a circular, flower-like pattern with the pointed ends facing outward. If desired, drizzle with a

touch of olive oil for added shine.

2. **Make the Garlic Aioli:**
   - In a small bowl, whisk together the mayonnaise, minced garlic, lemon juice, Dijon mustard, salt, and pepper until smooth and creamy. Adjust the seasoning to taste.

3. **Garnish and Serve:**
   - Garnish the artichoke petals with a sprinkle of chopped fresh parsley or dill, if using.
   - Place the garlic aioli in a small serving bowl in the center of the artichoke flower for easy dipping.
   - Serve immediately and enjoy.

Nutritional Information (Per Serving)

- Calories: 120
- Protein: 1g
- Fat: 12g
  - Saturated Fat: 1.5g
- Carbohydrates: 2g
  - Fiber: 1g
  - Sugar: 0g
- Sodium: 180mg
- Cholesterol: 8mg

The idea for Artichoke Heart Petals came to me while preparing appetizers for a springtime picnic. I wanted to create something visually stunning yet incredibly simple to prepare. As I was laying out the artichokes, the natural shape of the petals inspired me to arrange them like a blooming flower. Paired with a creamy garlic aioli, this dish became an instant crowd-pleaser.

I fondly remember serving it at a family gathering, where even those who were hesitant about artichokes couldn't resist trying it—and loving it! This appetizer is now a regular at my dinner parties, not only for its light, tangy flavor but also for the compliments it always earns for its elegant presentation. The combination of marinated artichokes and garlic aioli is proof that sometimes, the simplest dishes leave the biggest impression.

Notes

- *Artichoke Variations*: For a Mediterranean twist, sprinkle the petals with crumbled feta and a drizzle of olive oil.
- *Sauce Customization*: Mix in some harissa or smoked paprika to the aioli for a spicy or smoky variation.
- *Garnish Tips*: Add a sprinkle of toasted breadcrumbs over the petals for a crunchy texture.

Mushroom Ceviche

Serving Size: 4 servings

Prep Time: 15 minutes

Marination Time: 30 minutes

Total Time: 45 minutes

Ingredients

- 8 ounces white or cremini mushrooms, cleaned and thinly sliced
- 1/2 medium red onion, finely diced
- 1/4 cup fresh cilantro, chopped
- 1-2 jalapeños, seeded and finely diced (adjust for spice level)
- 3 limes, juiced (about 1/4 cup)
- 1 lemon, juiced (about 2 tablespoons)
- 1 small Roma tomato, finely diced
- 1 clove garlic, minced
- 1 tablespoon olive oil
- Salt and freshly ground black pepper (to taste)
- Optional: 1 avocado, diced, for garnish
- Tortilla chips or crackers, for serving

Instructions

1. **Prepare the Mushrooms:**
   - Thinly slice the mushrooms and place them in a medium-sized mixing bowl.
2. **Marinate the Mushrooms:**
   - Add the lime juice, lemon juice, and minced garlic to the bowl with the mushrooms. Toss to coat evenly.

- ○ Cover the bowl with plastic wrap and refrigerate for 30 minutes to allow the mushrooms to absorb the citrus flavors and slightly soften.

3. **Add the Vegetables and Herbs:**
    - ○ After marinating, add the diced red onion, cilantro, jalapeños, and tomato to the bowl. Drizzle with olive oil and season with salt and pepper to taste. Gently toss to combine.

4. **Garnish and Serve:**
    - ○ Transfer the mushroom ceviche to a serving bowl or platter. If desired, top with diced avocado for added creaminess.
    - ○ Serve immediately with tortilla chips or crackers on the side.

Nutritional Information (Per Serving)

- Calories: 80
- Protein: 2g
- Fat: 4g
    - ○ Saturated Fat: 0.5g
- Carbohydrates: 9g
    - ○ Fiber: 2g
    - ○ Sugar: 3g
- Sodium: 15mg
- Cholesterol: 0mg

Mushroom Ceviche was born from a moment of culinary curiosity. While traditional ceviche uses seafood, I wanted to create a plant-based version that retained the vibrant, zesty essence of the dish. Mushrooms, with their meaty texture and mild flavor, proved to be the perfect base for this experiment.

The first time I made this recipe, I brought it to a summer potluck. I watched as guests hesitated, intrigued by the concept of a "vegetarian ceviche," only to return for seconds and thirds. The bright lime juice, the heat from the jalapeños, and the fresh crunch of red onion and tomato made it an instant hit.

This dish has since become a favorite in my home, particularly for gatherings where dietary diversity is a must. It's refreshing, tangy, and surprisingly satisfying, embodying the spirit of ceviche in a unique, plant-based way. Every time I serve it, it sparks conversations and often steals the spotlight on the appetizer table.

Notes

- *Texture Tips*: For added crunch, garnish with toasted pumpkin seeds or chopped roasted almonds before serving.
- *Acid Balance*: If the citrus is too strong, a teaspoon of honey can balance the flavors beautifully.
- *Serving Variations*: Spoon the ceviche onto small endive leaves for an elegant, mess-free presentation.

Polenta Bites with Sundried Tomato Tapenade

Serving Size: 16 servings
Prep Time: 15 minutes
Cook Time: 20 minutes
Total Time: 35 minutes

Ingredients
For the Polenta:

- 1 tube (18 oz) of pre-cooked polenta, sliced into 16 even rounds (about 1/2-inch thick each)
- 1 tablespoon olive oil
- Salt and freshly ground black pepper (to taste)

For the Sundried Tomato Tapenade:

- 1/2 cup sundried tomatoes packed in oil, drained
- 1/4 cup pitted Kalamata olives
- 1 tablespoon capers, rinsed
- 1 clove garlic, minced
- 2 tablespoons fresh basil leaves
- 2 tablespoons olive oil
- 1 teaspoon fresh lemon juice
- Salt and freshly ground black pepper (to taste)

Optional Garnish:

- Fresh basil leaves
- Shaved Parmesan cheese

Instructions

1. **Prepare the Polenta Rounds:**
   - Slice the pre-cooked polenta into 16 even rounds. Pat them dry with a paper towel to remove excess moisture.
2. **Grill the Polenta:**
   - Heat a large skillet or grill pan over medium-high heat. Add the olive oil to the pan.
   - Place the polenta rounds in the skillet in a single layer. Cook for 4-5 minutes on each side, or until golden brown and crispy. Season with salt and pepper while cooking.
   - Transfer the grilled polenta rounds to a serving platter.
3. **Make the Sundried Tomato Tapenade:**
   - In a food processor, combine the sundried tomatoes, Kalamata olives, capers, garlic, and basil. Pulse until finely chopped.
   - With the food processor running, slowly drizzle in the olive oil and lemon juice until the mixture forms a smooth paste.
   - Taste and adjust seasoning with salt and pepper as needed.
4. **Assemble the Polenta Bites:**
   - Spoon a generous dollop of the sundried tomato tapenade onto each grilled polenta round.
   - Garnish with fresh basil leaves or shaved Parmesan cheese for added flavor and presentation.
5. **Serve:**
   - Serve immediately while the polenta rounds are warm, or at room temperature for a casual appetizer.

- Calories: 50
- Protein: 1g
- Fat: 3g
  - Saturated Fat: 0.5g
- Carbohydrates: 5g
  - Fiber: 1g
  - Sugar: 1g
- Sodium: 75mg
- Cholesterol: 0mg

Polenta Bites with Sundried Tomato Tapenade are a testament to the beauty of simple, bold flavors. This recipe was inspired by a trip to Tuscany, where I fell in love with the way Italian cuisine celebrates humble ingredients like polenta and sundried tomatoes. The rich, salty tapenade pairs perfectly with the crisp-edged, creamy polenta rounds, creating a bite-sized treat that's both rustic and refined.

The first time I served these was at a family holiday gathering, where they disappeared in minutes. My favorite part of making this dish is the reaction it gets—it looks so elegant that no one believes how easy it is to prepare. Now, these polenta bites are my go-to appetizer for entertaining, bringing a little taste of Italy to every table. Each bite is a reminder that sometimes, the simplest combinations create the most memorable dishes.

Notes

- *Polenta Tips*: For a crispy finish, fry the polenta rounds in a mix of butter and olive oil before topping with the tapenade.
- *Flavor Boost*: Add anchovies or roasted garlic to the tapenade for extra depth.

- *Serving Idea*: Arrange on a bed of arugula and drizzle with balsamic glaze for a more composed appetizer plate.

Cucumber Canvases

Serving Size: 24 servings
Prep Time: 20 minutes
Cook Time: 0 minutes
Total Time: 20 minutes

Ingredients

For the Cucumber Base:

- 2 large cucumbers
- 1 tablespoon lemon juice (to prevent browning, optional)

For the Herbed Cream Cheese:

- 8 ounces cream cheese, softened
- 1 tablespoon fresh dill, finely chopped
- 1 tablespoon fresh chives, finely chopped
- 1 teaspoon lemon zest
- 1 clove garlic, minced
- Salt and freshly ground black pepper (to taste)

Toppings:

- 4 ounces smoked salmon, cut into small, bite-sized pieces
- 2 tablespoons capers, rinsed and drained
- Optional garnish: additional dill sprigs or chive snippets

Instructions

1. **Prepare the Cucumber Base:**
   - Slice the cucumbers into 1/4-inch thick rounds or use a vegetable cutter to create artistic shapes (e.g., stars or flowers).

- Lay the cucumber slices on a paper towel to absorb excess moisture. Lightly brush with lemon juice if slicing ahead of time.

2. **Make the Herbed Cream Cheese:**
   - In a small mixing bowl, combine the softened cream cheese, dill, chives, lemon zest, minced garlic, salt, and pepper. Stir until smooth and evenly mixed.
   - Transfer the herbed cream cheese to a piping bag fitted with a decorative tip for a professional look, or use a small spoon for a rustic finish.

3. **Assemble the Cucumber Canvases:**
   - Pipe or spoon a dollop of herbed cream cheese onto each cucumber slice.
   - Top each slice with a small piece of smoked salmon. Add a caper or two to each for a salty burst of flavor.

4. **Garnish and Serve:**
   - Garnish the finished cucumber canvases with a sprig of dill or a snippet of chive for added flair.
   - Arrange on a serving platter and serve immediately. These can also be refrigerated for up to 2 hours before serving.

Nutritional Information (Per Serving)

- Calories: 35
- Protein: 2g
- Fat: 2.5g
  - Saturated Fat: 1.5g
- Carbohydrates: 1g
  - Fiber: 0g
  - Sugar: 0g

- Sodium: 90mg
- Cholesterol: 8mg

Cucumber Canvases were born out of a love for both art and entertaining. I wanted an appetizer that was as visually stunning as it was delicious, and the idea of using fresh, crisp cucumbers as an edible canvas felt like the perfect fit. The combination of herbed cream cheese, delicate smoked salmon, and briny capers creates a balanced bite that's creamy, fresh, and satisfying.

The first time I made these was for a friend's bridal shower, where they became the highlight of the appetizer spread. Guests couldn't stop complimenting the elegant presentation and refreshing flavor. What I love most about this recipe is its versatility—you can customize the shapes and toppings to match any occasion or theme. These cucumber canvases are not just appetizers; they're edible works of art that bring beauty and flavor to the table.

Notes

- *Vegetarian Options*: Replace the smoked salmon with thinly sliced avocado or roasted red peppers for a vegetarian-friendly option.
- *Creative Cuts*: Use cookie cutters to create unique shapes like hearts or stars from the cucumber slices.
- *Spice It Up*: Sprinkle the cream cheese with a pinch of smoked paprika or a dash of cayenne for a subtle kick.

Inspired Accompaniments

1. **Caprese Salad with Balsamic Glaze**: A classic Caprese salad featuring ripe tomatoes, fresh mozzarella, and basil leaves drizzled with a rich balsamic reduction.

2. **Mediterranean Couscous Salad**: A refreshing couscous salad with Mediterranean flavors, including cherry tomatoes, cucumber, Kalamata olives, feta cheese, and a lemon-herb dressing.

3. **Garlic-Parmesan Knots**: Soft and fluffy garlic-parmesan knots, perfect for dipping in marinara sauce or olive oil with herbs.

4. **Roasted Vegetable Platter**: An array of roasted seasonal vegetables served with a tahini-yogurt dipping sauce.

5. **Truffle Fries with Aioli**: Crispy truffle oil-infused french fries accompanied by a homemade garlic aioli.

6. **Spinach and Artichoke Dip**: A creamy spinach and artichoke dip, served with tortilla chips or crusty bread for dipping.

7. **Italian-Style Bruschetta**: Classic bruschetta with diced tomatoes, garlic, fresh basil, and a drizzle of extra virgin olive oil on toasted baguette slices.

8. **Lemon-Herb Quinoa**: Light and fluffy quinoa seasoned with lemon zest, fresh herbs, and roasted pine nuts.

9. **Roasted Garlic Hummus with Pita**: Silky roasted garlic hummus served with warm, toasted pita bread.

10. **Grilled Zucchini Ribbons**: Zucchini ribbons lightly grilled and drizzled with a lemon vinaigrette, garnished with toasted almonds and Parmesan shavings.

Caprese Salad with Balsamic Glaze

Serving Size: 4 servings
Prep Time: 10 minutes
Cook Time: 15 minutes
Total Time: 25 minutes

Ingredients
For the Salad:

- 4 large ripe tomatoes, sliced into 1/4-inch thick rounds
- 8 ounces fresh mozzarella, sliced into 1/4-inch thick rounds
- 1/4 cup fresh basil leaves
- 2 tablespoons extra virgin olive oil
- Salt and freshly ground black pepper (to taste)

For the Balsamic Glaze:

- 1/2 cup balsamic vinegar
- 1 tablespoon honey or brown sugar (optional, for added sweetness)

Instructions

1. **Prepare the Balsamic Glaze (if not store-bought):**
   - In a small saucepan, pour the balsamic vinegar. Add honey or brown sugar, if using, for sweetness.
   - Heat over medium heat and bring to a gentle simmer. Reduce the heat to low and let the mixture cook, stirring occasionally, until reduced by half and thickened to a syrupy consistency (about 10-15 minutes).
   - Remove from heat and let cool slightly. The glaze

will thicken further as it cools.

2. **Assemble the Salad:**
   - Arrange the tomato slices, mozzarella slices, and basil leaves alternately on a serving platter or individual plates, slightly overlapping them for a visually appealing presentation.
   - Drizzle the olive oil evenly over the salad.
   - Lightly sprinkle with salt and freshly ground black pepper to taste.

3. **Finish with the Balsamic Glaze:**
   - Drizzle the balsamic glaze over the tomatoes, mozzarella, and basil, using as much or as little as desired.
   - Serve immediately and enjoy the vibrant flavors of this classic Italian salad.

Nutritional Information (Per Serving)

- Calories: 220
- Protein: 9g
- Fat: 15g
  - Saturated Fat: 7g
- Carbohydrates: 10g
  - Fiber: 1g
  - Sugar: 6g
- Sodium: 200mg
- Cholesterol: 30mg

Caprese Salad with Balsamic Glaze holds a special place in my heart as a dish that embodies simplicity and elegance. I first encountered this salad during a summer trip to Italy, where I was captivated by the vibrant markets overflowing with ripe tomatoes and fragrant basil. The way the locals celebrated fresh, seasonal ingredients inspired me to recreate this dish at home.

The first time I made it, I was struck by how such minimal ingredients could yield such a harmonious and flavorful result. The creamy mozzarella, juicy tomatoes, and aromatic basil, all tied together by the tangy-sweet balsamic glaze, create a symphony of textures and tastes. It has since become my go-to dish for entertaining, as its stunning presentation and bold flavors always impress.

Every time I prepare this salad, I'm reminded of the warmth and simplicity of Italian cuisine. It's a celebration of fresh ingredients, perfect for a summer meal or as a vibrant appetizer to share with loved ones.

Notes

- *Tomato Choices*: Use a mix of heirloom tomatoes in varying colors (red, yellow, and green) for a vibrant and visually striking presentation.
- *Balsamic Glaze Shortcut*: If short on time, use a high-quality store-bought balsamic glaze. Add a pinch of sugar and gently heat for a personalized touch.
- *Cheese Options*: Swap mozzarella with burrata for a creamier texture or bocconcini (small mozzarella balls) for a bite-sized variation.
- *Pairing Suggestion*: Serve with warm crusty bread or garlic crostini to soak up the juices from the salad.

Mediterranean Couscous Salad

Serving Size: 6 servings
Prep Time: 15 minutes
Cook Time: 10 minutes
Total Time: 25 minutes

Ingredients
For the Salad:

- 1 cup couscous
- 1 1/4 cups vegetable or chicken broth
- 1 cup cherry tomatoes, halved
- 1 cup cucumber, diced
- 1/4 cup red onion, finely chopped
- 1/2 cup Kalamata olives, pitted and halved
- 1/2 cup crumbled feta cheese
- 1/4 cup fresh parsley, chopped
- 2 tablespoons fresh mint, chopped (optional)

For the Lemon-Herb Dressing:

- 3 tablespoons extra virgin olive oil
- 2 tablespoons fresh lemon juice
- 1 teaspoon lemon zest
- 1 teaspoon Dijon mustard
- 1 clove garlic, minced
- 1 teaspoon dried oregano
- Salt and freshly ground black pepper (to taste)

Instructions

1. **Cook the Couscous:**
   - Bring the broth to a boil in a medium saucepan.

Remove from heat, stir in the couscous, and cover.
Let it sit for 5 minutes to absorb the liquid.
  - Fluff the couscous with a fork and transfer it to a
large mixing bowl to cool slightly.

2. **Prepare the Lemon-Herb Dressing:**
   - In a small bowl or jar, whisk together the olive oil,
lemon juice, lemon zest, Dijon mustard, minced
garlic, dried oregano, salt, and pepper. Set aside.

3. **Assemble the Salad:**
   - Add the cherry tomatoes, cucumber, red onion,
Kalamata olives, and parsley to the couscous. Toss
gently to combine.
   - Drizzle the lemon-herb dressing over the salad
and toss again to coat evenly.

4. **Add the Feta Cheese:**
   - Gently fold in the crumbled feta cheese, being
careful not to break it apart too much.
   - Taste and adjust seasoning with additional salt,
pepper, or lemon juice as needed.

5. **Serve:**
   - Transfer the salad to a serving platter or bowl.
Garnish with additional parsley or mint if desired.
   - Serve immediately or refrigerate for up to 2 hours
for a chilled salad.

Nutritional Information (Per Serving)

- Calories: 210
- Protein: 6g
- Fat: 10g
  - Saturated Fat: 3g
- Carbohydrates: 24g
  - Fiber: 2g

- ◦ Sugar: 2g
- Sodium: 300mg
- Cholesterol: 10mg

Mediterranean Couscous Salad is a recipe that transports me to sun-soaked Mediterranean shores with every bite. Inspired by a family picnic at the beach, where light, refreshing meals were the highlight of the day, this dish became a staple in my kitchen for its simplicity and vibrant flavors.

The first time I made this salad, it was for a summer potluck. I remember how the bright colors of the tomatoes, cucumbers, and olives, combined with the zesty lemon dressing, caught everyone's attention. It became the most talked-about dish of the event, with friends asking for the recipe before the day was over.

What I love most about this salad is its versatility. It's perfect as a side dish for grilled meats, a light lunch, or even a vegetarian main course. Every forkful is a burst of fresh, tangy, and savory flavors, reminding me that the best dishes are often the simplest ones, crafted with care and love.

Notes

- *Couscous Alternatives*: Try substituting couscous with quinoa, farro, or bulgur for a heartier or gluten-free option.
- *Make It Ahead*: This salad tastes even better when made a few hours in advance, allowing the flavors to meld. Store in the refrigerator, but let it come to room temperature before serving.
- *Extra Texture*: Add toasted pine nuts or slivered almonds for a delightful crunch.
- *Serving Idea*: Serve alongside grilled chicken or fish for a light, Mediterranean-inspired meal.

Garlic-Parmesan Knots

Serving Size: 12 servings
Prep Time: 20 minutes
Cook Time: 15 minutes
Total Time: 35 minutes

Ingredients
For the Dough:

- 1 pound pizza dough (store-bought or homemade)
- All-purpose flour (for dusting)

For the Garlic-Parmesan Butter:

- 4 tablespoons unsalted butter, melted
- 2 cloves garlic, finely minced
- 1/4 cup grated Parmesan cheese
- 1 tablespoon fresh parsley, finely chopped
- 1/2 teaspoon Italian seasoning
- 1/4 teaspoon salt

For Dipping (Optional):

- 1 cup marinara sauce, warmed
- Extra virgin olive oil with Italian herbs

Instructions

1. **Prepare the Dough:**
   - Preheat your oven to 375°F (190°C) and line a baking sheet with parchment paper.
   - Lightly dust your work surface with flour and divide the pizza dough into 12 equal portions.

- Roll each portion into a rope about 6-8 inches long. Tie each rope into a knot, tucking the ends underneath.

2. **Prepare the Garlic-Parmesan Butter:**
   - In a small bowl, mix the melted butter, minced garlic, Parmesan cheese, parsley, Italian seasoning, and salt. Reserve half of the butter mixture for brushing after baking.

3. **Brush and Bake:**
   - Place the knots on the prepared baking sheet, spacing them about 1 inch apart.
   - Brush the tops of the knots generously with half of the garlic-Parmesan butter mixture.
   - Bake in the preheated oven for 12-15 minutes, or until the knots are golden brown and puffed.

4. **Finish with Butter:**
   - Remove the knots from the oven and immediately brush them with the remaining garlic-Parmesan butter mixture for an extra burst of flavor.

5. **Serve:**
   - Arrange the knots on a serving platter and serve warm with marinara sauce or olive oil with Italian herbs for dipping.

Nutritional Information (Per Serving)

- Calories: 120
- Protein: 3g
- Fat: 5g
  - Saturated Fat: 3g
- Carbohydrates: 15g
  - Fiber: 1g
  - Sugar: 1g

- Sodium: 180mg
- Cholesterol: 10mg

Garlic-Parmesan Knots bring back memories of family pizza nights, where the aroma of garlic butter and freshly baked bread filled the kitchen. They were always the first to disappear, often eaten straight from the baking sheet before the meal even started.

The first time I made these from scratch, I was nervous about working with dough. But as I tied each knot and brushed on the buttery mixture, I realized how simple and satisfying it was to create something so comforting. The combination of fluffy dough, garlicky butter, and Parmesan cheese is irresistible.

These knots have since become my go-to recipe for gatherings, whether as an appetizer, a side dish for pasta, or a snack for game nights. They're easy to make, endlessly customizable, and always met with requests for more. The best part? Watching friends and family dip them into marinara sauce, their smiles proof of just how satisfying these little knots of joy can be.

Notes

- *Dough Options*: If making dough from scratch, try infusing it with roasted garlic or Italian seasoning for added flavor.
- *Cheese Variations*: Sprinkle grated asiago or pecorino Romano for a more robust cheesy flavor.
- *Perfect for Dipping*: Serve with a trio of dips, such as marinara sauce, pesto, and garlic aioli, for a versatile snack.
- *Make-Ahead Tip*: Prepare the knots and freeze before baking. Bake directly from frozen, adding a few extra minutes to the cooking time.

Roasted Vegetable Platter with Tahini-Yogurt Dipping Sauce

Serving Size: 6 servings
Prep Time: 15 minutes
Cook Time: 25 minutes
Total Time: 40 minutes

Ingredients
For the Roasted Vegetables:

- 2 medium zucchini, sliced into thick rounds
- 1 red bell pepper, cut into large chunks
- 1 yellow bell pepper, cut into large chunks
- 1 medium eggplant, sliced into thick rounds
- 1 cup cherry tomatoes
- 1 red onion, cut into wedges
- 2 tablespoons olive oil
- 1 teaspoon garlic powder
- 1 teaspoon dried oregano
- 1/2 teaspoon smoked paprika
- Salt and freshly ground black pepper (to taste)

For the Tahini-Yogurt Dipping Sauce:

- 1/2 cup plain Greek yogurt
- 2 tablespoons tahini
- 1 tablespoon lemon juice
- 1 clove garlic, minced
- 1 teaspoon ground cumin
- Salt and freshly ground black pepper (to taste)
- Water (to thin, as needed)

Instructions

1. **Preheat the Oven:**
   - Preheat your oven to 425°F (220°C) and line two large baking sheets with parchment paper.
2. **Prepare the Vegetables:**
   - In a large mixing bowl, combine the zucchini, bell peppers, eggplant, cherry tomatoes, and red onion.
   - Drizzle with olive oil and sprinkle with garlic powder, oregano, smoked paprika, salt, and pepper. Toss to coat evenly.
3. **Roast the Vegetables:**
   - Spread the vegetables in a single layer on the prepared baking sheets.
   - Roast in the preheated oven for 20-25 minutes, flipping halfway through, until the vegetables are tender and slightly caramelized.
4. **Prepare the Tahini-Yogurt Sauce:**
   - In a small bowl, whisk together the Greek yogurt, tahini, lemon juice, minced garlic, cumin, salt, and pepper.
   - Add water, 1 teaspoon at a time, until the sauce reaches your desired consistency for dipping.
5. **Assemble the Platter:**
   - Arrange the roasted vegetables on a large serving platter.
   - Serve with the tahini-yogurt sauce in a small bowl in the center for dipping.
6. **Serve:**
   - Garnish with additional chopped parsley or a sprinkle of sesame seeds, if desired, and serve immediately.

Nutritional Information (Per Serving)

- Calories: 120
- Protein: 4g
- Fat: 6g
    - Saturated Fat: 1g
- Carbohydrates: 13g
    - Fiber: 4g
    - Sugar: 5g
- Sodium: 150mg
- Cholesterol: 3mg

The Roasted Vegetable Platter with Tahini-Yogurt Dipping Sauce was inspired by a trip to a bustling Mediterranean market. I was captivated by the vibrant array of fresh produce and the tantalizing aroma of spices in the air. This dish captures the essence of those market stalls—simple, flavorful, and brimming with the goodness of seasonal vegetables.

The first time I made this platter was for a summer potluck. It was a hit, with its rich variety of textures and flavors complemented perfectly by the creamy, nutty tahini-yogurt sauce. It quickly became a staple in my kitchen, not just as a crowd-pleasing appetizer but also as a versatile side dish.

What I love most about this recipe is its adaptability. You can use any vegetables you have on hand and tailor the spices to suit your mood. It's a dish that celebrates the beauty of wholesome ingredients, turning something as simple as roasted vegetables into a feast for both the eyes and the palate.

Notes

- *Vegetable Customization*: Adjust the vegetable selection based on what's in season. Sweet potatoes, brussels sprouts, or mushrooms make excellent additions in cooler months.

- *Dipping Sauce Variations*: Add a pinch of smoked paprika or turmeric to the tahini-yogurt sauce for a vibrant color and smoky flavor.
- *Serving Tip*: Serve the vegetables warm or at room temperature for easy hosting, making it a great make-ahead dish for gatherings.
- *Pairing Idea*: This dish pairs wonderfully with grilled meats, falafel, or a warm pita bread spread.

Truffle Fries with Aioli

Serving Size: 4 servings
Prep Time: 15 minutes
Cook Time: 30 minutes
Total Time: 45 minutes

Ingredients
For the Truffle Fries:

- 4 large russet potatoes, scrubbed and cut into 1/4-inch thick fries
- 2 tablespoons olive oil
- 1 teaspoon garlic powder
- 1 teaspoon smoked paprika
- 1 teaspoon salt
- 1/4 cup grated Parmesan cheese (optional)
- 2 tablespoons truffle oil
- 1 tablespoon chopped fresh parsley (for garnish)

For the Garlic Aioli:

- 1/2 cup mayonnaise
- 1 clove garlic, finely minced or grated
- 1 teaspoon lemon juice
- Salt and freshly ground black pepper (to taste)

Instructions

1. **Prepare the Potatoes:**
   - Preheat your oven to 425°F (220°C) and line two large baking sheets with parchment paper.
   - Cut the potatoes into 1/4-inch thick fries. Soak them in a bowl of cold water for 20 minutes to

remove excess starch, which helps them crisp up.

- ○ Drain the potatoes and pat them dry with a clean kitchen towel.

2. **Season and Bake the Fries:**
   - ○ In a large bowl, toss the potatoes with olive oil, garlic powder, smoked paprika, and salt. Spread them in a single layer on the prepared baking sheets, ensuring they do not overlap.
   - ○ Bake in the preheated oven for 25-30 minutes, flipping halfway through, until golden brown and crispy.

3. **Prepare the Garlic Aioli:**
   - ○ In a small bowl, whisk together the mayonnaise, minced garlic, lemon juice, salt, and black pepper. Cover and refrigerate until ready to serve.

4. **Add the Truffle Flavor:**
   - ○ Remove the fries from the oven and immediately drizzle with truffle oil. Toss gently to coat evenly.
   - ○ If using, sprinkle with grated Parmesan cheese and garnish with chopped parsley.

5. **Serve:**
   - ○ Transfer the fries to a serving platter and serve immediately with the garlic aioli on the side for dipping.

Nutritional Information (Per Serving)

- **Fries:**
  - ○ Calories: 260
  - ○ Protein: 4g
  - ○ Fat: 10g
    - ▪ Saturated Fat: 2g
  - ○ Carbohydrates: 40g

- Fiber: 4g
    - Sugar: 1g
  - Sodium: 320mg
- **Garlic Aioli (2 tablespoons):**
  - Calories: 100
  - Protein: 0g
  - Fat: 11g
    - Saturated Fat: 2g
  - Carbohydrates: 1g
  - Sodium: 80mg

Truffle Fries with Aioli was born out of a love for elevating simple comfort foods. The first time I had truffle fries was at a quaint bistro during a weekend getaway, and I was instantly captivated by their rich, earthy aroma and crisp perfection. I knew I had to recreate that experience at home.

The first batch I made was during a movie night with friends, and they were gone within minutes. The combination of golden, crispy fries infused with the luxurious aroma of truffle oil and the creamy, garlicky aioli made them irresistible.

What I love most about this recipe is how easy it is to prepare yet how indulgent it feels. The Parmesan and parsley garnish add a touch of sophistication, while the truffle oil elevates the humble potato to gourmet status. Every time I make these fries, I'm reminded that sometimes the simplest ingredients can create the most extraordinary dishes.

Notes

- *Potato Choices*: Yukon gold potatoes create a creamier interior, while russet potatoes result in crispier fries.
- *Truffle Oil Application*: Drizzle the truffle oil over the fries after baking to retain its aromatic flavor. Avoid cooking the

oil, as it can lose potency.

- *Customize the Aioli*: Mix in a touch of Dijon mustard or grated Parmesan for an elevated dipping sauce.
- *Make It Fancy*: Garnish with fresh thyme or rosemary sprigs for a gourmet presentation.

Spinach and Artichoke Dip

Serving Size: 8 servings
Prep Time: 10 minutes
Cook Time: 25 minutes
Total Time: 35 minutes

Ingredients
For the Dip:

- 1 (8-ounce) package cream cheese, softened
- 1/2 cup mayonnaise
- 1/2 cup sour cream
- 1 (10-ounce) package frozen chopped spinach, thawed and squeezed dry
- 1 (14-ounce) can artichoke hearts, drained and roughly chopped
- 1 cup shredded mozzarella cheese
- 1/2 cup grated Parmesan cheese
- 2 cloves garlic, minced
- 1/4 teaspoon crushed red pepper flakes (optional, for heat)
- Salt and freshly ground black pepper (to taste)

For Serving:

- Tortilla chips, pita chips, or crusty bread

Instructions

1. **Preheat the Oven:**
   - Preheat your oven to 375°F (190°C) and lightly grease a medium baking dish or oven-safe skillet.
2. **Prepare the Dip Mixture:**

- In a large mixing bowl, combine the softened cream cheese, mayonnaise, and sour cream until smooth.
- Stir in the spinach, artichoke hearts, minced garlic, mozzarella, Parmesan, red pepper flakes (if using), salt, and black pepper. Mix until well combined.

3. **Assemble and Bake:**
   - Transfer the mixture to the prepared baking dish, spreading it evenly.
   - Bake in the preheated oven for 20-25 minutes, or until the dip is hot and bubbly, with the top lightly golden.

4. **Serve:**
   - Remove from the oven and let cool slightly before serving.
   - Serve warm with tortilla chips, pita chips, or slices of crusty bread for dipping.

Nutritional Information (Per Serving)

- Calories: 220
- Protein: 6g
- Fat: 18g
  - Saturated Fat: 9g
- Carbohydrates: 7g
  - Fiber: 2g
  - Sugar: 1g
- Sodium: 320mg
- Cholesterol: 35mg

Spinach and Artichoke Dip is a dish that never fails to bring people together. It's a classic appetizer I first discovered at a potluck, where the warm, creamy dip quickly became the centerpiece of the table. I loved how its rich flavors paired perfectly with crunchy chips and bread, making it an instant crowd-pleaser.

The first time I made this dip at home, it was for a family game night. Watching everyone eagerly gather around the table to scoop up the hot, cheesy goodness was a memory I'll never forget. The slight tanginess from the artichokes, the creaminess of the cheese, and the hint of garlic make every bite irresistible.

What makes this dish special is its versatility. You can tweak the recipe by adding ingredients like jalapeños for heat, bacon for extra indulgence, or a sprinkle of breadcrumbs for a crispy topping. It's become my go-to appetizer for parties and casual gatherings, and every time I serve it, it's met with rave reviews. Spinach and Artichoke Dip is proof that comfort food can also be elevated and sophisticated.

Notes

- *Cheese Blend*: For a more complex flavor, mix in fontina or Gruyère along with the mozzarella and Parmesan.
- *Make It Spicy*: Add a dash of cayenne or a sprinkle of red pepper flakes for a hint of heat.
- *Serving Idea*: Use a hollowed-out sourdough bread bowl as a unique serving vessel, and toast the removed bread pieces for dipping.
- *Storage and Reheating*: Store leftovers in an airtight container in the fridge. Reheat in a small skillet or the oven for a freshly baked feel.

Italian-Style Bruschetta

Serving Size: 20 servings
Prep Time: 10 minutes
Cook Time: 10 minutes
Total Time: 20 minutes

Ingredients
For the Tomato Topping:

- 4 large ripe tomatoes, diced (about 2 cups)
- 3 cloves garlic, finely minced
- 1/4 cup fresh basil leaves, chopped
- 2 tablespoons extra virgin olive oil
- 1 tablespoon balsamic vinegar (optional, for extra flavor)
- Salt and freshly ground black pepper (to taste)

For the Baguette:

- 1 French baguette, sliced into 1/2-inch thick rounds (about 20 slices)
- 2 tablespoons olive oil
- 1 clove garlic, peeled (for rubbing on toasted bread)

Instructions

1. **Prepare the Tomato Topping:**
   - In a medium mixing bowl, combine the diced tomatoes, minced garlic, chopped basil, olive oil, balsamic vinegar (if using), salt, and black pepper. Stir well and let the mixture sit for 5-10 minutes to allow the flavors to meld.
2. **Toast the Baguette Slices:**
   - Preheat your oven to 400°F (200°C).

- ○ Arrange the baguette slices on a baking sheet and brush both sides lightly with olive oil.
  - ○ Toast in the preheated oven for 6-8 minutes, flipping halfway through, until golden brown and crisp.
  - ○ Remove from the oven and immediately rub the cut side of the peeled garlic clove onto one side of each toasted slice for a subtle garlic flavor.

3. **Assemble the Bruschetta:**
   - ○ Spoon the tomato mixture generously onto the garlic-rubbed side of each toasted baguette slice.
   - ○ Drizzle with additional olive oil if desired and sprinkle with a touch of salt for finishing.

4. **Serve:**
   - ○ Arrange the bruschetta on a serving platter and serve immediately as a fresh, flavorful appetizer.

Nutritional Information (Per Serving)

- Calories: 90
- Protein: 2g
- Fat: 4g
  - ○ Saturated Fat: 0.5g
- Carbohydrates: 11g
  - ○ Fiber: 1g
  - ○ Sugar: 1g
- Sodium: 110mg

Italian-Style Bruschetta is a dish that embodies simplicity and the joy of using fresh, high-quality ingredients. My love for this classic appetizer began during a trip to Tuscany, where I learned to appreciate the art of transforming ripe tomatoes and crusty bread into something magical.

The first time I made this bruschetta at home was for a summer gathering. I remember guests gathering around the platter, savoring the juicy tomatoes and fragrant basil on the crisp, garlicky baguette. It was a reminder that food doesn't need to be complicated to impress—it just needs to be prepared with care.

What I love most about this recipe is its versatility. It's perfect for casual dinners, elegant parties, or even as a light snack. The combination of flavors and textures—sweet tomatoes, bold garlic, fresh basil, and crunchy bread—is a celebration of the Mediterranean spirit. Every time I serve it, I'm reminded of those sunny afternoons in Tuscany, and it always brings a smile to my face.

Notes

- *Tomato Prep*: Let the diced tomatoes sit in a colander for 10 minutes to remove excess liquid, preventing soggy bread.
- *Herb Variations*: Try adding fresh oregano or thyme for a different herbal flavor.
- *Crostini Upgrade*: Rub the toasted bread slices with a raw garlic clove for an added layer of flavor before topping with the tomato mixture.
- *Serving Suggestion*: Serve with a drizzle of aged balsamic vinegar or a sprinkle of shaved Parmesan for a luxurious twist.

Lemon-Herb Quinoa

Serving Size: 6 servings
Prep Time: 10 minutes
Cook Time: 15 minutes
Total Time: 25 minutes

Ingredients
For the Quinoa:

- 1 cup quinoa, rinsed
- 2 cups water or vegetable broth
- 1/2 teaspoon salt (if using water)

For the Lemon-Herb Seasoning:

- 1 tablespoon extra virgin olive oil
- Zest of 1 lemon
- 2 tablespoons fresh lemon juice
- 1/4 cup fresh parsley, chopped
- 2 tablespoons fresh dill or mint, chopped (optional)
- 1/4 teaspoon black pepper (or to taste)

For the Garnish:

- 1/4 cup roasted pine nuts
- 1 tablespoon extra parsley or dill, chopped (optional)

Instructions

1. **Cook the Quinoa:**
   - In a medium saucepan, bring the water or vegetable broth to a boil. Stir in the rinsed quinoa and 1/2 teaspoon salt if using water.

- ○ Reduce the heat to low, cover, and simmer for 12-15 minutes, or until the quinoa is tender and the liquid is absorbed.
  - ○ Remove from heat, fluff the quinoa with a fork, and let it sit uncovered for a few minutes to cool slightly.

2. **Prepare the Lemon-Herb Seasoning:**
   - ○ In a small bowl, whisk together the olive oil, lemon zest, lemon juice, parsley, dill or mint, and black pepper. Adjust seasoning to taste.

3. **Toast the Pine Nuts:**
   - ○ Heat a dry skillet over medium heat. Add the pine nuts and toast them, stirring frequently, for 2-3 minutes or until they are golden brown and fragrant. Remove from heat and set aside.

4. **Combine and Garnish:**
   - ○ Transfer the cooked quinoa to a large mixing bowl. Drizzle the lemon-herb seasoning over the quinoa and toss gently to combine.
   - ○ Sprinkle the toasted pine nuts over the quinoa and garnish with additional parsley or dill, if desired.

5. **Serve:**
   - ○ Serve warm or at room temperature as a light side dish or a base for a protein-packed main course.

Nutritional Information (Per Serving)

- Calories: 190
- Protein: 5g
- Fat: 6g
  - ○ Saturated Fat: 1g
- Carbohydrates: 27g

  - Fiber: 3g
  - Sugar: 1g
- Sodium: 120mg

Lemon-Herb Quinoa is one of those dishes that I love for its versatility and freshness. The idea for this recipe came to me while planning a picnic menu. I wanted a side dish that was light, packed with flavor, and easy to transport. Quinoa, with its fluffy texture and nutty flavor, was the perfect canvas for vibrant lemon and herbs.

The first time I made this dish, it was an instant hit with my family. The brightness of the lemon combined with the fresh parsley and the crunch of toasted pine nuts made it stand out among the other dishes. It's become a staple in my home, especially during the warmer months when fresh herbs are abundant.

What makes this recipe special is how adaptable it is. You can mix in seasonal vegetables, add feta cheese, or even use it as a base for grilled fish or chicken. Every time I serve it, I'm reminded of how simple ingredients, when thoughtfully combined, can create something truly memorable.

Notes

- *Cooking Tips*: Rinse quinoa thoroughly under cold water before cooking to remove its natural bitterness.
- *Nutrient Boost*: Add chopped spinach, kale, or arugula to the warm quinoa for a fresh, nutrient-packed salad.
- *Citrus Twist*: Substitute the lemon with lime or orange for a new flavor profile.
- *Pairing Idea*: Serve as a side dish with grilled salmon or roasted chicken for a light and zesty meal.

Roasted Garlic Hummus with Pita

Serving Size: 6 servings
Prep Time: 10 minutes
Cook Time: 35 minutes
Total Time: 45 minutes

Ingredients
For the Roasted Garlic:

- 1 whole garlic bulb
- 1 teaspoon olive oil
- Pinch of salt

For the Hummus:

- 1 (15-ounce) can chickpeas, drained and rinsed
- 2 tablespoons tahini
- Juice of 1 large lemon (about 2 tablespoons)
- 2 tablespoons olive oil (plus extra for garnish)
- 1 teaspoon ground cumin
- 1/2 teaspoon paprika (optional, for garnish)
- Salt and freshly ground black pepper (to taste)
- Water (as needed, for desired consistency)

For the Pita:

- 4 large pita breads
- 1 tablespoon olive oil
- Sprinkle of za'atar or dried oregano (optional, for seasoning)

Instructions

1. **Roast the Garlic:**
   - Preheat your oven to 400°F (200°C).
   - Slice the top off the garlic bulb to expose the cloves slightly. Drizzle with olive oil and sprinkle with a pinch of salt. Wrap the bulb in aluminum foil and roast for 30-35 minutes, or until the cloves are soft and golden brown.
   - Let the roasted garlic cool slightly, then squeeze the softened cloves out of their skins.
2. **Prepare the Hummus:**
   - In a food processor, combine the chickpeas, tahini, roasted garlic cloves, lemon juice, olive oil, ground cumin, salt, and pepper. Blend until smooth, scraping down the sides as needed.
   - Add water, 1 tablespoon at a time, until the hummus reaches your desired creamy consistency.
3. **Toast the Pita Bread:**
   - Preheat a grill pan or skillet over medium heat. Brush each pita bread lightly with olive oil and sprinkle with za'atar or oregano if desired.
   - Toast the pita for 1-2 minutes per side, or until warm and slightly crisp. Cut into wedges for serving.
4. **Assemble and Serve:**
   - Transfer the hummus to a serving bowl and drizzle with extra olive oil. Sprinkle with paprika for garnish, if desired.
   - Serve with the warm pita wedges on the side.

Nutritional Information (Per Serving)

- **Hummus:**
  - Calories: 180

- Protein: 5g
- Fat: 10g
  - Saturated Fat: 1.5g
- Carbohydrates: 16g
  - Fiber: 4g
  - Sugar: 1g
- Sodium: 180mg

- **Pita (1/4 large pita):**
  - Calories: 80
  - Protein: 3g
  - Fat: 2g
    - Saturated Fat: 0.3g
  - Carbohydrates: 13g
    - Fiber: 1g
    - Sugar: 1g
  - Sodium: 120mg

Roasted Garlic Hummus with Pita is a dish that never fails to bring a sense of warmth and comfort to my table. The inspiration for this recipe came from my love of Middle Eastern cuisine, where the simplest ingredients are transformed into something extraordinary with the right techniques.

The first time I made roasted garlic hummus, I was amazed at how the caramelized garlic added a rich, sweet depth to the creamy hummus. Pairing it with warm, toasted pita bread elevated the experience, making it feel like a restaurant-quality appetizer at home.

This recipe has become a staple at family gatherings and casual dinners with friends. It's perfect for dipping, spreading, or even as part of a mezze platter. What I love most is its versatility—you can customize the hummus with spices, herbs, or even roasted red peppers for variety. Every time I prepare this dish, I'm reminded of how food has the power to connect people, sparking conversation and creating moments of joy around the table.

Notes

- *Homemade Pita Chips*: Make your own pita chips by cutting pita bread into wedges, brushing with olive oil, and baking at 375°F (190°C) until crispy.
- *Flavor Variations*: Add roasted red peppers, sun-dried tomatoes, or jalapeños to the hummus for a flavorful twist.
- *Serving Tip*: Garnish with a drizzle of olive oil, a sprinkle of paprika, and toasted pine nuts for a professional touch.
- *Make It a Platter*: Pair the hummus with an assortment of vegetables like cucumber, carrots, and celery for a complete snack board.

Grilled Zucchini Ribbons with Lemon Vinaigrette

Serving Size: 4 servings
Prep Time: 15 minutes
Cook Time: 5 minutes
Total Time: 20 minutes

Ingredients
For the Zucchini Ribbons:

- 4 medium zucchinis, trimmed
- 1 tablespoon olive oil
- Salt and freshly ground black pepper (to taste)

For the Lemon Vinaigrette:

- 2 tablespoons extra virgin olive oil
- 1 tablespoon fresh lemon juice
- 1 teaspoon lemon zest
- 1 teaspoon Dijon mustard
- 1 clove garlic, finely minced
- Salt and freshly ground black pepper (to taste)

For the Garnish:

- 1/4 cup sliced almonds, toasted
- 1/4 cup Parmesan shavings (use a vegetable peeler)
- Fresh parsley or basil leaves (optional)

Instructions

1. **Prepare the Zucchini Ribbons:**
   - Use a vegetable peeler or mandoline to slice the

zucchinis into long, thin ribbons.

- ◦ Place the ribbons in a bowl and drizzle with 1 tablespoon olive oil. Toss gently to coat and season with salt and pepper.

2. **Grill the Zucchini:**
   - ◦ Preheat a grill pan or outdoor grill over medium-high heat.
   - ◦ Grill the zucchini ribbons in batches, laying them flat on the grill. Cook for 1-2 minutes per side, or until grill marks appear and the zucchini is tender but not mushy.
   - ◦ Transfer the grilled ribbons to a serving platter.

3. **Make the Lemon Vinaigrette:**
   - ◦ In a small bowl, whisk together the olive oil, lemon juice, lemon zest, Dijon mustard, minced garlic, salt, and pepper until emulsified. Adjust seasoning to taste.

4. **Assemble the Dish:**
   - ◦ Drizzle the lemon vinaigrette over the warm grilled zucchini ribbons.
   - ◦ Sprinkle the toasted almonds and Parmesan shavings evenly over the top.
   - ◦ Garnish with fresh parsley or basil leaves, if desired.

5. **Serve:**
   - ◦ Serve immediately as a light, refreshing side dish or appetizer.

Nutritional Information (Per Serving)

- Calories: 120
- Protein: 4g
- Fat: 9g

- ○ Saturated Fat: 2g
- Carbohydrates: 6g
  - ○ Fiber: 2g
  - ○ Sugar: 3g
- Sodium: 150mg

Grilled Zucchini Ribbons with Lemon Vinaigrette is one of those recipes that makes the most of simple, fresh ingredients. This dish was inspired by a summer barbecue where I wanted to create a lighter, vegetable-forward side dish to balance out heavier grilled meats. The idea of turning zucchini into delicate ribbons felt both elegant and approachable.

The first time I served this dish, it was an instant hit. The light char from the grill enhanced the natural sweetness of the zucchini, while the zesty lemon vinaigrette and crunchy toasted almonds added layers of flavor and texture. The Parmesan shavings were the final touch, lending a savory richness that tied everything together.

What I love most about this recipe is its versatility. It's perfect for summer gatherings, potlucks, or even a quick weeknight side dish. The vibrant flavors and beautiful presentation always draw compliments, proving that sometimes the simplest dishes are the most memorable. This recipe reminds me of the joy in celebrating fresh, seasonal produce and the power of thoughtful seasoning.

Notes

- *Tool Tip*: Use a mandoline or vegetable peeler to ensure uniform zucchini ribbons for even cooking.
- *Enhance the Flavor*: Add a drizzle of aged balsamic vinegar or honey for a sweet-savory balance.
- *Alternative Nuts*: Substitute almonds with toasted hazelnuts or pine nuts for a new flavor profile.
- *Serving Suggestion*: Serve as a side dish for grilled fish or as

a topping for pasta or grain bowls for added freshness.

106

Signature Pizzas

1. **Edible Flower Garden Pizza**: Create a garden-inspired pizza with colorful edible flowers, fresh herbs, and a creamy goat cheese base.

2. **Thai-Inspired Coconut Curry Pizza**: Infuse your pizza with Thai flavors by using coconut curry sauce, shrimp, fresh basil, and bean sprouts.

3. **Mediterranean Mezze Platter Pizza**: Transform your pizza into a Mediterranean feast with hummus, roasted red peppers, olives, feta, and tzatziki drizzle.

4. **Sushi-Inspired Seafood Pizza**: Craft a sushi-inspired pizza with thinly sliced sashimi-grade fish, seaweed salad, avocado, and a drizzle of soy-ginger sauce.

5. **Tandoori Chicken Naan Pizza**: Turn naan bread into a pizza canvas and top it with tandoori-spiced chicken, yogurt sauce, and fresh cucumber salad.

6. **Smoked Salmon and Caviar Pizza**: Elevate your pizza with luxurious Ingredients like smoked salmon, crème fraîche, and a garnish of caviar.

7. **BBQ Pulled Pork and Pineapple Pizza**: Combine the flavors of BBQ pulled pork, sweet pineapple, red onions, and cheddar cheese for a smoky-sweet delight.

8. **Vegan Cauliflower Crust Mediterranean Pizza**: Craft a vegan pizza using a cauliflower crust and load it with roasted vegetables, vegan cheese, and tahini drizzle.

9. **Moroccan Spiced Lamb and Harissa Pizza**: Spice up your pizza with Moroccan-seasoned ground lamb, harissa sauce, roasted bell peppers, and mint yogurt drizzle.

10. **Breakfast for Dinner Pancake Pizza**: Get creative with a breakfast-inspired pizza by using a pancake base, scrambled eggs, bacon, maple syrup, and a sprinkle of cheddar cheese.

Edible Flower Garden Pizza

Serving Size: 8 servings
Prep Time: 20 minutes
Cook Time: 15 minutes
Total Time: 35 minutes

Ingredients
For the Pizza Base:

- 1 pizza dough (store-bought or homemade)
- 1 tablespoon olive oil
- 1 teaspoon garlic powder

For the Goat Cheese Spread:

- 8 ounces goat cheese, softened
- 2 tablespoons heavy cream or milk (to thin, if needed)
- 1 tablespoon fresh chives, finely chopped
- 1 tablespoon fresh basil, finely chopped
- Salt and freshly ground black pepper (to taste)

For the Toppings:

- 1/2 cup edible flowers (e.g., pansies, nasturtiums, violas, or marigold petals)
- 1/4 cup fresh basil leaves
- 1/4 cup fresh parsley or dill sprigs
- 1/4 cup thinly sliced radishes (optional, for crunch)
- 1/4 teaspoon flaky sea salt (optional, for garnish)

Instructions

1. **Prepare the Pizza Base:**

- Preheat your oven to 475°F (245°C) or follow the instructions for your pizza dough.
- Roll out the pizza dough on a floured surface to your desired shape and thickness. Transfer to a parchment-lined baking sheet or pizza stone.
- Brush the dough lightly with olive oil and sprinkle with garlic powder for added flavor.
- Par-bake the crust for 5-7 minutes until just set but not browned.

2. **Make the Goat Cheese Spread:**
   - In a mixing bowl, combine the softened goat cheese, heavy cream (if needed for spreadability), chopped chives, chopped basil, salt, and pepper. Mix until smooth and creamy.

3. **Assemble the Pizza:**
   - Remove the par-baked crust from the oven and allow it to cool slightly.
   - Spread the goat cheese mixture evenly over the crust, leaving a small border around the edges.

4. **Bake the Pizza:**
   - Return the pizza to the oven and bake for another 7-10 minutes, or until the crust is golden and the goat cheese is warmed through.

5. **Add the Edible Flower Garden:**
   - Once the pizza has slightly cooled, carefully arrange the edible flowers, fresh basil leaves, parsley, and any optional toppings like radish slices over the goat cheese base. Sprinkle with flaky sea salt, if desired, for added texture and flavor.

6. **Serve:**
   - Slice the pizza into pieces and serve immediately,

enjoying the vibrant colors and fresh, herbaceous flavors.

Nutritional Information (Per Serving)

- Calories: 190
- Protein: 7g
- Fat: 9g
  - Saturated Fat: 5g
- Carbohydrates: 18g
  - Fiber: 1g
  - Sugar: 1g
- Sodium: 250mg
- Cholesterol: 15mg

Edible Flower Garden Pizza was inspired by a sunny afternoon spent in my grandmother's garden. Surrounded by vibrant blooms and the fragrant scent of herbs, I wanted to capture that essence in a dish. This pizza is not just food—it's an artistic expression of nature's beauty.

The first time I made this pizza was for a small gathering of friends. I remember the "oohs" and "aahs" as the colorful edible flowers were unveiled. Many were skeptical about eating flowers but were quickly converted after their first bite. The creamy goat cheese pairs beautifully with the freshness of the herbs and the subtle floral notes.

This dish has since become a favorite for spring and summer parties. It's more than just a meal; it's a centerpiece that celebrates the seasons and turns simple ingredients into something extraordinary. Every slice feels like a bite of a garden in full bloom.

Notes

- *Edible Flower Tips*: Ensure the flowers you use are culinary-grade and pesticide-free. Pansies, nasturtiums, and marigold petals are not only visually stunning but also add unique, subtle flavors.

- *Goat Cheese Options*: Substitute with ricotta for a milder flavor or whipped feta for added creaminess and tang.
- *Seasonal Variations*: Add seasonal toppings like shaved zucchini in summer or roasted squash in autumn to complement the edible flowers.
- *Presentation*: Arrange the flowers just before serving to ensure they stay vibrant and fresh. Serve this pizza as the centerpiece of a spring or summer brunch for maximum visual impact.

Thai-Inspired Coconut Curry Pizza

Serving Size: 8 servings
Prep Time: 20 minutes
Cook Time: 15 minutes
Total Time: 35 minutes

Ingredients
For the Pizza Base:

- 1 pizza dough (store-bought or homemade)
- 1 tablespoon olive oil

For the Coconut Curry Sauce:

- 1/2 cup canned coconut milk
- 1 tablespoon red curry paste (adjust for spice level)
- 1 teaspoon fish sauce (optional, for umami)
- 1 teaspoon sugar
- 1 teaspoon lime juice

Toppings:

- 1 cup cooked shrimp, peeled and deveined
- 1/2 cup shredded mozzarella cheese
- 1/2 cup bean sprouts
- 1/4 cup thinly sliced red bell pepper
- 1/4 cup fresh basil leaves (Thai basil preferred)
- 2 tablespoons chopped fresh cilantro
- 1 tablespoon crushed peanuts (optional, for garnish)
- Lime wedges (optional, for serving)

Instructions

1. **Prepare the Coconut Curry Sauce:**
   - In a small saucepan, combine the coconut milk, red curry paste, fish sauce (if using), sugar, and lime juice.
   - Heat over medium heat, stirring constantly, until the mixture is smooth and slightly thickened (about 5 minutes). Set aside to cool slightly.
2. **Prepare the Pizza Dough:**
   - Preheat your oven to 475°F (245°C) or follow the instructions for your pizza dough.
   - Roll out the pizza dough on a floured surface to your desired shape and thickness. Transfer to a parchment-lined baking sheet or pizza stone.
   - Lightly brush the dough with olive oil.
3. **Assemble the Pizza:**
   - Spread the coconut curry sauce evenly over the pizza dough, leaving a small border around the edges.
   - Sprinkle the shredded mozzarella cheese over the sauce.
   - Evenly distribute the cooked shrimp and thinly sliced red bell pepper over the cheese.
4. **Bake the Pizza:**
   - Bake the pizza in the preheated oven for 12-15 minutes, or until the crust is golden brown and the cheese is melted and bubbly.
5. **Add Fresh Toppings:**
   - Remove the pizza from the oven and let it cool slightly. Top with bean sprouts, fresh basil leaves, cilantro, and crushed peanuts (if using).
6. **Serve:**
   - Slice the pizza into pieces and serve with lime

wedges on the side for an extra burst of citrus flavor.

Nutritional Information (Per Serving)

- Calories: 210
- Protein: 10g
- Fat: 8g
    - Saturated Fat: 4g
- Carbohydrates: 22g
    - Fiber: 2g
    - Sugar: 3g
- Sodium: 320mg
- Cholesterol: 45mg

Thai-Inspired Coconut Curry Pizza was created as a fusion of two of my favorite cuisines—Italian and Thai. One rainy evening, craving the warmth of Thai curry but the comfort of pizza, I decided to combine the two. The result was a vibrant and aromatic dish that perfectly blends creamy coconut curry sauce with the classic appeal of pizza.

The first time I served this pizza was for a movie night with friends. The bold flavors and unique toppings were a hit, with everyone reaching for seconds. The shrimp adds a touch of elegance, while the fresh basil and bean sprouts keep it light and refreshing. Lime wedges on the side bring everything together with a citrusy pop.

This pizza has since become a staple for casual gatherings, offering a fun twist on traditional pizza that never fails to impress. It's a delicious reminder that experimenting in the kitchen often leads to the best dishes.

Notes

- *Protein Variations*: Swap shrimp for shredded chicken, tofu, or even thinly sliced beef, depending on your preference.
- *Sauce Tips*: Make the sauce spicier by adding extra curry paste or a splash of sriracha. For a milder option, use yellow curry paste instead of red.
- *Fresh Toppings*: Bean sprouts and crushed peanuts should be added just before serving to retain their crunch.
- *Pairing Idea*: Pair with a light Thai iced tea or a crisp lager to balance the richness of the curry flavors.

Mediterranean Mezze Platter Pizza

Serving Size: 8 servings
Prep Time: 20 minutes
Cook Time: 15 minutes
Total Time: 35 minutes

Ingredients
For the Pizza Base:

- 1 pizza dough (store-bought or homemade)
- 1 tablespoon olive oil

For the Toppings:

- 1/2 cup hummus (store-bought or homemade)
- 1/2 cup roasted red peppers, sliced
- 1/4 cup Kalamata olives, pitted and sliced
- 1/4 cup crumbled feta cheese
- 1/2 cup cherry tomatoes, halved
- 1/4 teaspoon dried oregano (optional, for garnish)

For the Tzatziki Drizzle:

- 1/2 cup Greek yogurt
- 1 tablespoon cucumber, finely grated and squeezed dry
- 1 teaspoon fresh dill, chopped
- 1 teaspoon lemon juice
- 1 small clove garlic, minced
- Salt and freshly ground black pepper (to taste)

Instructions

1. **Prepare the Pizza Dough:**

- Preheat your oven to 475°F (245°C) or follow the instructions for your pizza dough.
- Roll out the dough on a floured surface to your desired shape and thickness. Transfer to a parchment-lined baking sheet or pizza stone.
- Brush the dough lightly with olive oil and bake for 5-7 minutes, or until lightly golden.

2. **Prepare the Tzatziki Drizzle:**
   - In a small bowl, mix the Greek yogurt, grated cucumber, dill, lemon juice, garlic, salt, and pepper. Stir until smooth and set aside in the refrigerator to chill.

3. **Assemble the Pizza:**
   - Remove the par-baked crust from the oven and allow it to cool slightly.
   - Spread a thin, even layer of hummus over the crust, leaving a small border around the edges.
   - Top with sliced roasted red peppers, Kalamata olives, crumbled feta cheese, and halved cherry tomatoes.

4. **Bake the Pizza:**
   - Return the pizza to the oven and bake for another 8-10 minutes, or until the crust is golden and the toppings are heated through.

5. **Finish with Tzatziki Drizzle:**
   - Remove the pizza from the oven and let it cool slightly. Drizzle the prepared tzatziki sauce over the top.
   - Sprinkle with dried oregano or additional dill for garnish, if desired.

6. **Serve:**
   - Slice the pizza and serve immediately, enjoying

the fresh, bold Mediterranean flavors.

Nutritional Information (Per Serving)

- Calories: 180
- Protein: 6g
- Fat: 8g
  - Saturated Fat: 3g
- Carbohydrates: 20g
  - Fiber: 2g
  - Sugar: 2g
- Sodium: 280mg
- Cholesterol: 10mg

The Mediterranean Mezze Platter Pizza was inspired by my love for mezze platters—those vibrant spreads of hummus, olives, roasted vegetables, and pita bread that turn any gathering into a feast. I wanted to capture that variety and freshness in a pizza, and the result was a delightful fusion of flavors and textures.

I first made this pizza for a weekend brunch with friends. The creamy hummus base, tangy feta, and briny olives were perfectly balanced by the refreshing tzatziki drizzle. Each bite was like a mini mezze platter, and it quickly became the star of the table.

This pizza is not only a crowd-pleaser but also a versatile recipe that can be tailored to your favorite Mediterranean ingredients. Whether it's a casual dinner or a celebratory gathering, this dish brings a taste of the Mediterranean to any occasion, with minimal effort and maximum flavor.

Notes

- *Hummus Base Tips*: For added depth, mix in roasted garlic or smoked paprika into the hummus before spreading it on the crust.

- *Tzatziki Variation*: If you don't have time to make tzatziki, use plain Greek yogurt with a sprinkle of dill and lemon zest.
- *Customization*: Add grilled eggplant, artichokes, or sliced cucumber for more Mediterranean flair.
- *Serving Suggestion*: Cut into smaller slices and serve alongside a mezze platter with dolmas and pita chips for a complete spread.

Sushi-Inspired Seafood Pizza

Serving Size: 8 servings
Prep Time: 25 minutes
Cook Time: 10 minutes
Total Time: 35 minutes

Ingredients
For the Pizza Base:

- 1 pizza dough (store-bought or homemade)
- 1 tablespoon sesame oil

For the Toppings:

- 4 ounces sashimi-grade fish (e.g., tuna, salmon, or yellowtail), thinly sliced
- 1/2 cup seaweed salad
- 1/2 avocado, thinly sliced
- 1/4 cup thinly sliced cucumber
- 1 teaspoon black sesame seeds
- 1 teaspoon white sesame seeds
- 2 green onions, thinly sliced (optional)

For the Soy-Ginger Sauce:

- 1/4 cup soy sauce
- 1 tablespoon rice vinegar
- 1 teaspoon sesame oil
- 1 teaspoon grated fresh ginger
- 1 teaspoon honey or sugar (optional, for sweetness)

Instructions

1. **Prepare the Soy-Ginger Sauce:**
   - In a small bowl, whisk together the soy sauce, rice vinegar, sesame oil, grated ginger, and honey or sugar (if using). Set aside to allow the flavors to meld.

2. **Prepare the Pizza Base:**
   - Preheat your oven to 475°F (245°C) or follow the instructions for your pizza dough.
   - Roll out the dough on a floured surface to your desired shape and thickness. Transfer to a parchment-lined baking sheet or pizza stone.
   - Lightly brush the dough with sesame oil to enhance the sushi-inspired flavor.
   - Bake the crust for 8-10 minutes, or until lightly golden and crisp. Allow to cool slightly before adding toppings.

3. **Assemble the Sushi-Inspired Toppings:**
   - Spread the seaweed salad evenly over the cooled pizza crust as a flavorful base.
   - Arrange the thinly sliced sashimi-grade fish, avocado, and cucumber over the seaweed salad. Create a visually appealing pattern for a sushi-inspired presentation.

4. **Garnish and Drizzle:**
   - Sprinkle the pizza with black and white sesame seeds for added texture.
   - Drizzle the soy-ginger sauce lightly over the pizza, reserving extra on the side for dipping or additional drizzling.
   - Garnish with thinly sliced green onions, if desired.

5. **Serve:**

- Slice the pizza and serve immediately. Enjoy it as a fresh, sushi-inspired take on pizza that's perfect for seafood lovers.

Nutritional Information (Per Serving)

- Calories: 200
- Protein: 10g
- Fat: 7g
  - Saturated Fat: 1g
- Carbohydrates: 22g
  - Fiber: 2g
  - Sugar: 1g
- Sodium: 420mg
- Cholesterol: 15mg

Sushi-Inspired Seafood Pizza was born from a playful experiment in combining my love for sushi with my passion for pizza. It started as a creative challenge to blend two iconic cuisines, and the result was a stunning dish that feels indulgent and fresh all at once.

The first time I made this pizza was for a family dinner, where it quickly became a conversation starter. The sashimi-grade fish, creamy avocado, and tangy soy-ginger sauce struck the perfect balance of flavor and texture. Even skeptics of "fusion food" were won over after one bite.

What I love most about this dish is its versatility. You can customize the toppings with your favorite sushi ingredients, like pickled ginger or tobiko, to make it your own. This pizza is not just a meal—it's an experience that transforms sushi night into something unexpected and delightful. It's my go-to when I want to impress guests or simply treat myself to a unique culinary creation.

Notes

- *Fish Selection*: Ensure your fish is sashimi-grade for safety and optimal flavor. You can mix and match fish like tuna, salmon, and yellowtail for variety.
- *Sauce Customization*: Add wasabi or a touch of yuzu juice to the soy-ginger sauce for a zesty kick.
- *Visual Appeal*: Arrange toppings in a colorful, geometric pattern to mimic the aesthetic of sushi rolls.
- *Perfect Pairing*: Serve with a side of miso soup or a small seaweed salad to complete the sushi-inspired experience.

Tandoori Chicken Naan Pizza

Serving Size: 4 servings
Prep Time: 20 minutes
Cook Time: 15 minutes
Total Time: 35 minutes

Ingredients
For the Tandoori Chicken:

- 1 boneless, skinless chicken breast (about 8 ounces), cubed
- 1/4 cup plain yogurt
- 1 tablespoon lemon juice
- 1 teaspoon tandoori masala spice blend
- 1/2 teaspoon ground cumin
- 1/2 teaspoon paprika
- 1/4 teaspoon ground turmeric
- 1 clove garlic, minced
- 1 teaspoon grated fresh ginger
- Salt and freshly ground black pepper (to taste)

For the Pizza:

- 2 pieces naan bread
- 1 tablespoon olive oil
- 1/2 cup shredded mozzarella cheese (optional, for fusion style)

For the Yogurt Sauce:

- 1/2 cup plain Greek yogurt
- 1 teaspoon lemon juice
- 1/2 teaspoon ground cumin
- 1/2 teaspoon garlic powder

- Salt and freshly ground black pepper (to taste)

For the Fresh Cucumber Salad:

- 1/2 cucumber, diced
- 1/4 cup red onion, finely chopped
- 1 tablespoon fresh cilantro, chopped
- 1 teaspoon lemon juice
- Salt and freshly ground black pepper (to taste)

Instructions

1. **Prepare the Tandoori Chicken:**
   - In a medium bowl, combine the yogurt, lemon juice, tandoori masala, cumin, paprika, turmeric, garlic, ginger, salt, and pepper. Add the chicken cubes and toss to coat thoroughly.
   - Marinate in the refrigerator for at least 15 minutes (or up to 2 hours for deeper flavor).
2. **Cook the Tandoori Chicken:**
   - Heat a skillet over medium-high heat and add a drizzle of olive oil.
   - Cook the marinated chicken pieces for 6-8 minutes, turning occasionally, until fully cooked and slightly charred. Remove from heat and set aside.
3. **Prepare the Yogurt Sauce:**
   - In a small bowl, whisk together the Greek yogurt, lemon juice, cumin, garlic powder, salt, and pepper. Refrigerate until ready to use.
4. **Make the Cucumber Salad:**
   - In another bowl, combine the diced cucumber, red onion, cilantro, lemon juice, salt, and pepper.

Toss to mix and set aside.

5. **Assemble the Naan Pizzas:**
   - Preheat your oven to 400°F (200°C).
   - Brush the naan bread lightly with olive oil. If using mozzarella cheese, sprinkle a thin layer on top of the naan for a fusion-style pizza.
   - Arrange the cooked tandoori chicken evenly on the naan.
6. **Bake the Pizzas:**
   - Place the naan pizzas on a baking sheet and bake for 10-12 minutes, or until the naan is crisp and the cheese (if using) is melted.
7. **Top and Serve:**
   - Remove the pizzas from the oven and drizzle generously with the yogurt sauce.
   - Add spoonfuls of the fresh cucumber salad on top for a refreshing crunch.
   - Slice and serve immediately.

Nutritional Information (Per Serving)

- Calories: 320
- Protein: 22g
- Fat: 12g
  - Saturated Fat: 3g
- Carbohydrates: 32g
  - Fiber: 2g
  - Sugar: 4g
- Sodium: 450mg
- Cholesterol: 55mg

Tandoori Chicken Naan Pizza was inspired by a memorable meal at a small fusion bistro where Indian flavors were playfully combined with classic pizza elements. Wanting to recreate that experience at home, I decided to use naan as the pizza base, embracing its soft, pillowy texture and authentic flavor.

The first time I served this dish was during a family movie night, and it quickly became a favorite. The tandoori chicken's smoky spices, creamy yogurt sauce, and crisp cucumber salad created a perfect harmony of flavors and textures. Everyone loved how the naan held up to the toppings, making it easy to enjoy without utensils.

What I love most about this recipe is its adaptability. You can add your own twist with toppings like sliced jalapeños or a drizzle of mango chutney. It's a dish that brings together bold flavors and simple preparation, making it perfect for weeknights or casual gatherings. Every time I make it, I'm reminded of the joy that comes from blending culinary traditions.

Notes

- *Chicken Variations*: Use leftover grilled chicken or rotisserie chicken if short on time. For vegetarians, swap chicken for paneer or roasted cauliflower.
- *Extra Spice*: For a bolder flavor, drizzle a bit of tamarind chutney or mint chutney over the pizza before serving.
- *Serving Suggestion*: Cut into wedges and serve alongside mango lassi or chai tea for a well-rounded Indian-inspired meal.
- *Make-Ahead Tip*: The tandoori chicken can be pre-cooked and stored in the fridge for up to 2 days to save time.

Smoked Salmon and Caviar Pizza

Serving Size: 8 servings
Prep Time: 20 minutes
Cook Time: 10 minutes
Total Time: 30 minutes

Ingredients
For the Pizza Base:

- 1 pizza dough (store-bought or homemade)
- 1 tablespoon olive oil

For the Toppings:

- 1/2 cup crème fraîche
- 4 ounces smoked salmon, thinly sliced
- 1/4 small red onion, thinly sliced
- 1 tablespoon fresh dill, chopped
- 1 teaspoon capers, drained
- 1-2 teaspoons high-quality caviar (e.g., salmon roe or sturgeon caviar)
- Freshly ground black pepper (to taste)
- Lemon wedges (optional, for serving)

Instructions

1. **Prepare the Pizza Base:**
   - Preheat your oven to 475°F (245°C) or follow the instructions for your pizza dough.
   - Roll out the pizza dough on a floured surface to your desired shape and thickness. Transfer to a parchment-lined baking sheet or pizza stone.
   - Brush the dough lightly with olive oil to help

achieve a golden, crisp crust.

2. **Bake the Pizza Base:**
    - Bake the dough for 8-10 minutes, or until the crust is golden brown and cooked through. Remove from the oven and let it cool slightly.
3. **Add the Crème Fraîche Base:**
    - Once the crust has cooled slightly, spread a thin, even layer of crème fraîche over the surface, leaving a small border around the edges.
4. **Layer the Toppings:**
    - Arrange the smoked salmon slices evenly over the crème fraîche.
    - Sprinkle the red onion slices, chopped dill, and capers over the salmon.
5. **Garnish with Caviar:**
    - Add small dollops of caviar evenly across the pizza for a luxurious touch.
    - Finish with a sprinkle of freshly ground black pepper for added flavor.
6. **Serve:**
    - Slice the pizza and serve immediately. For an extra burst of freshness, serve with lemon wedges on the side for optional drizzling.

Nutritional Information (Per Serving)

- Calories: 220
- Protein: 9g
- Fat: 11g
    - Saturated Fat: 4g
- Carbohydrates: 22g
    - Fiber: 1g
    - Sugar: 1g

- Sodium: 320mg
- Cholesterol: 30mg

Smoked Salmon and Caviar Pizza was inspired by a trip to a seaside town where fresh seafood was the star of every meal. I wanted to recreate the luxurious flavors of smoked salmon and caviar in a way that felt approachable yet indulgent. Combining these classic ingredients with the familiar comfort of pizza turned out to be a winning idea.

The first time I made this dish was for a celebratory brunch. The creamy crème fraîche, salty capers, and rich caviar balanced perfectly with the smoky salmon and crisp crust. It became an instant favorite, with guests marveling at the elegance and simplicity of the recipe.

What I love most about this pizza is its versatility. It works equally well as an appetizer for a dinner party or the centerpiece of a sophisticated brunch. Each bite feels like a special treat, reminding me that a little indulgence can turn an ordinary meal into something extraordinary.

Notes

- *Caviar Tips*: Use salmon roe for a budget-friendly option or sturgeon caviar for a luxurious touch.
- *Flavor Enhancers*: Add a sprinkle of lemon zest or dill-infused olive oil to brighten the flavors.
- *Presentation*: Slice the pizza into small squares or triangles for an elegant appetizer at cocktail parties.
- *Pairing Idea*: Complement this dish with a glass of Champagne or a crisp white wine like Sauvignon Blanc.

BBQ Pulled Pork and Pineapple Pizza

Serving Size: 8 servings
    Prep Time: 20 minutes
    Cook Time: 15 minutes
    Total Time: 35 minutes

Ingredients
For the Pizza Base:

- 1 pizza dough (store-bought or homemade)
- 1 tablespoon olive oil

For the Toppings:

- 1/2 cup barbecue sauce (plus extra for drizzling)
- 1 cup cooked pulled pork
- 1 cup fresh pineapple chunks (or canned, drained)
- 1/2 cup thinly sliced red onion
- 1 cup shredded cheddar cheese
- 1/2 cup shredded mozzarella cheese
- 1 tablespoon fresh cilantro, chopped (optional, for garnish)

Instructions

1. **Prepare the Pizza Base:**
   - Preheat your oven to 475°F (245°C) or follow the instructions for your pizza dough.
   - Roll out the dough on a floured surface to your desired shape and thickness. Transfer to a parchment-lined baking sheet or pizza stone.
   - Lightly brush the surface with olive oil for a crisp crust.

2. **Assemble the Pizza:**
   - Spread an even layer of barbecue sauce over the pizza dough, leaving a small border around the edges.
   - Evenly distribute the pulled pork, pineapple chunks, and red onion slices over the sauce.
   - Sprinkle the cheddar cheese and mozzarella cheese evenly over the toppings.
3. **Bake the Pizza:**
   - Place the pizza in the preheated oven and bake for 12-15 minutes, or until the crust is golden brown and the cheese is melted and bubbly.
4. **Finish with Garnish:**
   - Remove the pizza from the oven and let it cool slightly. Drizzle with a bit more barbecue sauce if desired.
   - Garnish with fresh chopped cilantro for a burst of color and flavor.
5. **Serve:**
   - Slice and serve immediately while the pizza is warm and the cheese is gooey.

Nutritional Information (Per Serving)

- Calories: 280
- Protein: 12g
- Fat: 11g
  - Saturated Fat: 5g
- Carbohydrates: 30g
  - Fiber: 1g
  - Sugar: 8g
- Sodium: 450mg
- Cholesterol: 30mg

BBQ Pulled Pork and Pineapple Pizza is the result of my love for combining sweet and savory flavors. It was inspired by a backyard barbecue where I couldn't decide between enjoying the pulled pork sandwiches or the grilled pineapple skewers. The idea of combining these elements on a pizza struck me as the perfect solution.

The first time I made this pizza, it was a hit with friends who loved the smoky richness of the pulled pork paired with the sweet tang of pineapple. The barbecue sauce acts as a bold and flavorful base, while the cheddar and mozzarella create that irresistible, melty finish.

What I love most about this pizza is its versatility—it feels indulgent yet fun, making it perfect for casual gatherings or game nights. Every bite is a balance of textures and flavors, reminding me of the joy of summer barbecues and good times with loved ones.

Notes

- *Flavor Boost*: Use smoked gouda or pepper jack cheese instead of cheddar for a more intense flavor profile.
- *Custom BBQ Sauce*: Create your own sauce by mixing equal parts ketchup, apple cider vinegar, brown sugar, and a touch of smoked paprika.
- *Pineapple Twist*: For an extra depth of flavor, caramelize the pineapple chunks in a skillet before adding them to the pizza.
- *Serving Suggestion*: Serve with coleslaw on the side for a true barbecue experience.

Vegan Cauliflower Crust Mediterranean Pizza

Serving Size: 8 servings
Prep Time: 30 minutes
Cook Time: 25 minutes
Total Time: 55 minutes

Ingredients
For the Cauliflower Crust:

- 1 medium head of cauliflower (about 4 cups, riced)
- 1/4 cup ground flaxseed + 3/4 cup water (flax egg substitute)
- 1/2 cup almond flour
- 1 teaspoon garlic powder
- 1 teaspoon dried oregano
- 1/2 teaspoon salt

For the Toppings:

- 1/2 cup hummus (as the base sauce)
- 1/2 cup roasted red peppers, sliced
- 1/2 cup cherry tomatoes, halved
- 1/4 cup Kalamata olives, pitted and sliced
- 1/4 cup red onion, thinly sliced
- 1/2 cup vegan mozzarella or feta-style cheese
- 1 tablespoon olive oil
- Fresh basil or parsley, chopped (optional, for garnish)

For the Tahini Drizzle:

- 2 tablespoons tahini
- 1 tablespoon lemon juice

- 1 tablespoon water (to thin, as needed)
- 1/4 teaspoon garlic powder
- Pinch of salt

Instructions

1. **Prepare the Cauliflower Crust:**
   - Preheat your oven to 400°F (200°C) and line a baking sheet with parchment paper.
   - Rice the cauliflower by grating it with a box grater or pulsing it in a food processor until it resembles fine crumbs.
   - Microwave the riced cauliflower for 5 minutes, then let it cool. Transfer to a clean kitchen towel and squeeze out as much moisture as possible to ensure a crispy crust.
   - In a large bowl, combine the cauliflower, flax egg (flaxseed mixed with water and allowed to sit for 5 minutes), almond flour, garlic powder, oregano, and salt. Mix until it forms a dough-like consistency.
   - Shape the mixture into a pizza crust (about 1/4-inch thick) on the prepared baking sheet. Bake for 20 minutes or until golden brown and firm to the touch.
2. **Prepare the Toppings:**
   - While the crust bakes, roast the vegetables. Toss cherry tomatoes, red onion, and roasted red peppers with olive oil and a pinch of salt. Spread on a separate baking sheet and roast in the oven for 10-12 minutes.
   - Whisk together the tahini, lemon juice, garlic powder, salt, and water to create a smooth,

drizzle-able sauce. Adjust consistency with more water if needed.

3. **Assemble the Pizza:**
   - Remove the baked cauliflower crust from the oven and let it cool slightly. Spread a thin layer of hummus over the crust as the base sauce.
   - Evenly distribute the roasted vegetables, olives, and vegan cheese on top.

4. **Final Bake:**
   - Return the pizza to the oven and bake for an additional 5-7 minutes, or until the cheese is melted and toppings are warmed through.

5. **Finish and Serve:**
   - Drizzle the tahini sauce over the pizza and garnish with fresh basil or parsley, if desired.
   - Slice and serve immediately, enjoying the blend of creamy, tangy, and savory Mediterranean flavors.

Nutritional Information (Per Serving)

- Calories: 120
- Protein: 4g
- Fat: 7g
  - Saturated Fat: 1g
- Carbohydrates: 10g
  - Fiber: 3g
  - Sugar: 2g
- Sodium: 220mg
- Cholesterol: 0mg

Vegan Cauliflower Crust Mediterranean Pizza was born out of a desire to create a dish that was both health-conscious and packed with Mediterranean flavors. The first time I made this pizza, it was for a friend who had recently gone vegan, and I wanted to show her that plant-based meals could be just as indulgent and satisfying as their traditional counterparts.

The crispy cauliflower crust, paired with the creamy hummus and roasted vegetables, creates a delightful balance of textures and flavors. The tahini drizzle ties everything together with its nutty and tangy notes, elevating the dish to something truly special.

What I love most about this pizza is its versatility. It's a blank canvas that can be tailored to include your favorite vegetables or vegan cheeses. Every time I make it, I'm reminded of how easy it is to create something both nourishing and delicious without compromising on flavor. This pizza is a testament to the joy of cooking creatively, proving that eating plant-based can be both exciting and deeply satisfying.

Notes

- *Cauliflower Crust Tips*: To ensure a firm crust, be thorough when squeezing out the moisture from the cauliflower. This step is critical for achieving the desired texture.
- *Tahini Drizzle Variations*: Add a hint of smoked paprika or turmeric to the tahini drizzle for a colorful and flavorful twist.
- *Add More Greens*: Garnish with a handful of fresh arugula or spinach for added freshness and crunch.
- *Storage Tip*: Leftover slices can be stored in an airtight container in the fridge and reheated in the oven to maintain the crispiness of the crust.

Moroccan Spiced Lamb and Harissa Pizza

Serving Size: 8 servings
Prep Time: 20 minutes
Cook Time: 15 minutes
Total Time: 35 minutes

Ingredients
For the Pizza Base:

- 1 pizza dough (store-bought or homemade)
- 1 tablespoon olive oil

For the Lamb Topping:

- 1/2 pound ground lamb
- 1 teaspoon ground cumin
- 1 teaspoon ground coriander
- 1/2 teaspoon ground cinnamon
- 1/2 teaspoon paprika
- 1/4 teaspoon cayenne pepper (optional, for heat)
- 1 clove garlic, minced
- Salt and freshly ground black pepper (to taste)

For the Toppings:

- 1/4 cup harissa sauce
- 1/2 cup roasted red bell peppers, sliced
- 1/4 cup thinly sliced red onion
- 1/2 cup crumbled feta cheese
- 1/4 cup chopped fresh parsley or cilantro (optional, for garnish)

For the Mint Yogurt Drizzle:

- 1/2 cup plain Greek yogurt
- 1 tablespoon fresh mint, finely chopped
- 1 teaspoon lemon juice
- Salt and freshly ground black pepper (to taste)

Instructions

1. **Prepare the Pizza Dough:**
   - Preheat your oven to 475°F (245°C) or follow the instructions for your pizza dough.
   - Roll out the dough on a floured surface to your desired shape and thickness. Transfer to a parchment-lined baking sheet or pizza stone.
   - Lightly brush the surface of the dough with olive oil.

2. **Cook the Spiced Lamb:**
   - Heat a skillet over medium-high heat and add a drizzle of olive oil.
   - Add the ground lamb and cook for 2-3 minutes, breaking it into small crumbles with a wooden spoon.
   - Stir in the cumin, coriander, cinnamon, paprika, cayenne (if using), garlic, salt, and pepper. Cook for an additional 3-4 minutes, or until the lamb is browned and fully cooked. Remove from heat and set aside.

3. **Assemble the Pizza:**
   - Spread the harissa sauce evenly over the pizza dough, leaving a small border around the edges.
   - Distribute the spiced lamb evenly over the sauce.
   - Add the roasted red bell peppers, red onion slices,

and crumbled feta cheese.

4. **Bake the Pizza:**
    - Place the pizza in the oven and bake for 12-15 minutes, or until the crust is golden brown and the toppings are heated through.

5. **Prepare the Mint Yogurt Drizzle:**
    - In a small bowl, whisk together the Greek yogurt, chopped mint, lemon juice, salt, and pepper. Adjust the consistency with a splash of water if needed for drizzling.

6. **Finish and Serve:**
    - Remove the pizza from the oven and let it cool slightly. Drizzle with the mint yogurt sauce and garnish with fresh parsley or cilantro, if desired.
    - Slice and serve immediately, enjoying the bold, spiced flavors.

Nutritional Information (Per Serving)

- Calories: 280
- Protein: 12g
- Fat: 13g
    - Saturated Fat: 5g
- Carbohydrates: 24g
    - Fiber: 2g
    - Sugar: 3g
- Sodium: 360mg
- Cholesterol: 35mg

Moroccan Spiced Lamb and Harissa Pizza is a dish that combines my love for bold, global flavors with the comforting appeal of pizza. This recipe was inspired by a trip to Marrakech, where the vibrant spices and earthy harissa left a lasting impression on my palate.

The first time I made this pizza, it was for a small dinner party. I remember watching my guests marvel at the unique combination of flavors—the warm, spiced lamb, the smoky sweetness of roasted peppers, and the cooling mint yogurt drizzle. It quickly became the highlight of the evening, with everyone asking for the recipe.

What I love most about this pizza is its balance. The harissa sauce provides heat and depth, while the mint yogurt drizzle adds a refreshing, creamy finish. It's a dish that feels adventurous yet familiar, perfect for anyone looking to spice up their pizza night with a touch of Moroccan flair. Every bite takes me back to the bustling markets and aromatic spice stalls that inspired it.

Notes

- *Lamb Tips*: If lamb is unavailable, substitute with ground beef or turkey seasoned with the same spices.
- *Harissa Heat*: Adjust the level of heat by adding more or less harissa to the base sauce. For extra complexity, mix harissa with a touch of honey.
- *Serving Idea*: Pair with a side of mint tea or a Moroccan-style salad with orange slices and olives for a complete meal.
- *Presentation*: Garnish with toasted almonds or pomegranate seeds for an additional Moroccan touch.

Breakfast for Dinner Pancake Pizza

Serving Size: 4 servings
Prep Time: 15 minutes
Cook Time: 20 minutes
Total Time: 35 minutes

Ingredients
For the Pancake Base:

- 1 cup all-purpose flour
- 1 tablespoon sugar
- 1 teaspoon baking powder
- 1/4 teaspoon baking soda
- 1/4 teaspoon salt
- 1 large egg
- 1 cup buttermilk
- 1 tablespoon unsalted butter, melted
- 1 teaspoon vanilla extract
- 1 tablespoon butter (for cooking the pancake)

For the Toppings:

- 4 large eggs, scrambled
- 4 strips cooked bacon, crumbled
- 1/2 cup shredded cheddar cheese
- 2 tablespoons chopped fresh chives (optional, for garnish)
- 2 tablespoons maple syrup (for drizzling)

Instructions

1. **Prepare the Pancake Base Batter:**
   - In a medium mixing bowl, whisk together the flour, sugar, baking powder, baking soda, and salt.

- In a separate bowl, whisk together the egg, buttermilk, melted butter, and vanilla extract.
   - Gradually add the wet ingredients to the dry ingredients, whisking until just combined. Do not overmix; lumps are okay.
2. **Cook the Pancake Base:**
   - Heat a large nonstick skillet or griddle over medium heat and melt 1 tablespoon of butter.
   - Pour the pancake batter into the skillet to form a large, pizza-sized round. Spread gently to achieve an even thickness.
   - Cook for 2-3 minutes, or until bubbles form on the surface and the edges start to set. Carefully flip and cook for another 2-3 minutes, or until golden brown and cooked through. Transfer to a baking sheet or oven-safe plate.
3. **Prepare the Scrambled Eggs:**
   - In a small bowl, whisk the eggs with a pinch of salt and pepper.
   - Heat a nonstick skillet over medium-low heat and add a drizzle of butter or oil.
   - Pour in the whisked eggs and cook, stirring gently, until soft and creamy. Remove from heat.
4. **Assemble the Pancake Pizza:**
   - Preheat your oven to 375°F (190°C).
   - Spread the scrambled eggs evenly over the pancake base.
   - Sprinkle the crumbled bacon and shredded cheddar cheese on top.
5. **Bake the Pancake Pizza:**
   - Place the pancake pizza in the oven and bake for 5-7 minutes, or until the cheese is melted and

bubbly.

6. **Finish with Maple Syrup and Garnish:**
   - Drizzle the pancake pizza with maple syrup and garnish with fresh chives, if desired.
   - Slice into wedges and serve immediately.

Nutritional Information (Per Serving)

- Calories: 310
- Protein: 13g
- Fat: 15g
  - Saturated Fat: 7g
- Carbohydrates: 31g
  - Fiber: 1g
  - Sugar: 6g
- Sodium: 480mg
- Cholesterol: 155mg

Breakfast for Dinner Pancake Pizza was inspired by a weekend tradition in my house: pancake breakfasts. One evening, craving both breakfast and the comfort of pizza, I decided to merge the two. The idea of a giant pancake as the base for savory breakfast toppings was both playful and practical—and it turned out to be a delicious hit.

The first time I served this dish was during a family movie night, where its whimsical presentation stole the show. The fluffy pancake base, creamy scrambled eggs, crispy bacon, and gooey cheddar cheese drizzled with maple syrup created a perfect balance of sweet and savory.

What I love most about this recipe is its adaptability. You can easily swap bacon for sausage, add sautéed vegetables, or even use plant-based alternatives to make it vegetarian. Every time I make it, I'm reminded that food can be both creative and comforting, turning simple ingredients into something truly special.

Notes

- *Custom Toppings*: Swap bacon for crumbled sausage or vegetarian alternatives like plant-based sausage or roasted mushrooms.
- *Syrup Choices*: Use flavored syrups, such as maple-bourbon or cinnamon-infused, for a unique twist.
- *Creative Additions*: Add dollops of whipped ricotta or mascarpone for an extra layer of indulgence.

- *Kid-Friendly Idea*: Make smaller pancake pizzas and let kids add their own toppings for a fun, interactive meal.

Global Fusion Pizzas

1. **Korean BBQ Beef Pizza**: A bold combination of tender Korean-style beef, tangy kimchi, and a sweet-spicy gochujang sauce base.

2. **Mexican Street Corn Pizza**: Inspired by the flavors of elote, this pizza features a creamy, tangy base with roasted corn and zesty lime.

3. **Greek Spanakopita Pizza**: A playful nod to the classic Greek spinach pie, featuring spinach, feta, and flaky phyllo-inspired crust textures.

4. **Indian Butter Chicken Pizza**: Creamy butter chicken served atop a naan-style pizza crust, delivering a rich and aromatic flavor profile.

5. **Japanese Teriyaki Salmon Pizza**: A light and flavorful pizza featuring tender teriyaki-glazed salmon, crisp vegetables, and a sesame kick.

6. **Moroccan Vegetable Tagine Pizza**: This vegan-friendly pizza highlights the rich, spiced flavors of a Moroccan tagine with roasted vegetables and harissa.

7. **Thai Peanut Chicken Pizza**: A savory-sweet delight that brings the flavors of a Thai peanut stir-fry to your pizza plate.

8. **Caribbean Jerk Shrimp Pizza**: Tropical flavors shine in this spicy and tangy shrimp pizza with sweet pineapple and zesty jerk seasoning.

9. **French Ratatouille Pizza**: A rustic yet elegant pizza inspired by the classic Provençal vegetable dish, with a vibrant medley of fresh produce.

10. **Hawaiian Poke Pizza**: A refreshing twist on the classic Hawaiian pizza, incorporating fresh ahi tuna, avocado, and a soy-ginger glaze.

Korean BBQ Beef Pizza

Serving Size: 4 servings
Prep Time: 20 minutes
Cook Time: 12-15 minutes
Total Time: 35 minutes

Ingredients
For the Bulgogi Beef:

- 1/2 pound thinly sliced ribeye or sirloin beef
- 2 tablespoons soy sauce
- 1 tablespoon sesame oil
- 1 tablespoon brown sugar
- 1 teaspoon grated ginger
- 2 garlic cloves, minced
- 1 teaspoon rice vinegar
- 1/4 teaspoon black pepper

For the Gochujang Barbecue Sauce:

- 2 tablespoons gochujang (Korean chili paste)
- 1/4 cup ketchup
- 1 tablespoon soy sauce
- 1 tablespoon honey
- 1 teaspoon sesame oil
- 1 teaspoon rice vinegar

For the Pizza Base:

- 1 pizza dough (store-bought or homemade)
- 1 tablespoon olive oil

Toppings:

- 1 1/2 cups shredded mozzarella cheese
- 1/2 cup kimchi, drained and chopped
- 2 scallions, thinly sliced
- 1 tablespoon toasted sesame seeds

For the Sriracha Mayo Drizzle:

- 2 tablespoons mayonnaise
- 1 teaspoon sriracha (adjust to taste)
- 1 teaspoon lime juice

Instructions

Prepare the Bulgogi Beef:

1. In a bowl, combine soy sauce, sesame oil, brown sugar, ginger, garlic, rice vinegar, and black pepper. Mix well.
2. Add the thinly sliced beef to the marinade, ensuring it is fully coated. Let it marinate for at least 15 minutes (or up to 1 hour for deeper flavor).
3. Heat a skillet over medium-high heat. Cook the beef slices in batches for 2-3 minutes per side until caramelized and cooked through. Set aside.

Prepare the Gochujang Barbecue Sauce:

1. In a small saucepan over medium heat, combine gochujang, ketchup, soy sauce, honey, sesame oil, and rice vinegar. Stir well and simmer for 2-3 minutes until the sauce thickens slightly. Set aside to cool.

Assemble the Pizza:

1. Preheat your oven to 475°F (245°C) and place a pizza stone or baking sheet inside to heat.

2. Roll out the pizza dough on a floured surface to your desired thickness. Transfer the dough to a piece of parchment paper for easy handling.
3. Brush the dough with olive oil, then spread an even layer of the gochujang barbecue sauce over the surface, leaving a small border around the edges.
4. Sprinkle the shredded mozzarella cheese evenly over the sauce.
5. Distribute the cooked bulgogi beef and chopped kimchi over the cheese.

Bake the Pizza:

1. Carefully transfer the pizza (with the parchment paper) to the preheated stone or baking sheet.
2. Bake for 12-15 minutes, or until the crust is golden and the cheese is melted and bubbly.

Add Finishing Touches:

1. Remove the pizza from the oven and let it cool slightly.
2. Sprinkle the pizza with sliced scallions and toasted sesame seeds.
3. In a small bowl, mix mayonnaise, sriracha, and lime juice. Drizzle the sriracha mayo over the pizza for a creamy, spicy finish.

Serve: Slice and serve immediately. Pair with an icy cold lager or a sparkling water infused with lime for a refreshing complement.

Nutritional Information (Per Serving)

- Calories: 420
- Protein: 22g
- Fat: 18g

- Saturated Fat: 8g
- Carbohydrates: 42g
- Fiber: 2g
- Sugar: 9g
- Sodium: 850mg

This Korean BBQ Beef Pizza was born out of my love for fusion cuisine and a lingering memory of my first experience with Korean bulgogi. It was during a trip to a bustling Seoul night market where I tasted bulgogi wrapped in crispy lettuce and paired with kimchi. The rich, caramelized beef and tangy kimchi left such a lasting impression that I knew I had to recreate those flavors at home.

One evening, craving both pizza and those bold Korean flavors, I decided to combine the two. The result was nothing short of magical—a pizza that captured the sweet, spicy, and savory essence of bulgogi while staying true to the cheesy comfort of a classic pie. It has since become a household favorite, especially for casual gatherings. I love watching my friends' faces light up when they take their first bite, the unexpected combination of kimchi and melted mozzarella creating an unforgettable moment.

This dish reminds me that food has the power to blend cultures and create something entirely new—one bite, and you're transported across the globe.

Notes

- *Meat Alternatives*: Swap beef with thinly sliced chicken or tofu for a lighter or vegetarian option.
- *Extra Crunch*: Add shredded carrots or radish slices for added texture and freshness.
- *Heat Level*: Adjust the spiciness by adding more gochujang or sriracha to suit your taste.

Mexican Street Corn Pizza

Serving Size: 4 servings
Prep Time: 20 minutes
Cook Time: 12-15 minutes
Total Time: 35 minutes

Ingredients
For the Lime Crema Base:

- 1/2 cup sour cream
- 2 tablespoons mayonnaise
- 1 tablespoon lime juice
- 1 teaspoon lime zest
- 1/4 teaspoon garlic powder
- Salt to taste

For the Toppings:

- 1 cup roasted corn kernels (fresh, frozen, or canned, drained)
- 1 1/2 cups shredded mozzarella cheese
- 1/4 cup Cotija cheese, crumbled
- 1-2 jalapeños, thinly sliced (seeds removed for less heat)
- 1 teaspoon chili powder
- 2 tablespoons chopped fresh cilantro

For the Pizza Base:

- 1 pizza dough (store-bought or homemade)
- 1 tablespoon olive oil

Optional Garnish:

- Lime wedges for serving
- Extra chili powder or Tajín for sprinkling

Instructions
Prepare the Lime Crema:

1. In a small bowl, mix the sour cream, mayonnaise, lime juice, lime zest, garlic powder, and salt until smooth. Adjust seasoning as needed. Set aside.

Roast the Corn:

1. Heat a skillet over medium-high heat. Add the corn kernels (if using fresh corn, cut them off the cob first).
2. Cook for 5-7 minutes, stirring occasionally, until the corn is golden and slightly charred. Remove from heat and set aside.

Assemble the Pizza:

1. Preheat your oven to 475°F (245°C) and place a pizza stone or baking sheet inside to heat.
2. Roll out the pizza dough on a floured surface to your desired thickness. Transfer the dough to a piece of parchment paper for easy handling.
3. Brush the dough lightly with olive oil, then spread an even layer of the lime crema over the surface, leaving a small border around the edges.
4. Sprinkle the shredded mozzarella evenly over the lime crema.
5. Distribute the roasted corn, sliced jalapeños, and crumbled Cotija cheese over the pizza. Sprinkle chili powder evenly across the toppings for added flavor.

Bake the Pizza:

1. Carefully transfer the pizza (with the parchment paper) onto the preheated stone or baking sheet.
2. Bake for 12-15 minutes, or until the crust is golden and the cheese is melted and bubbly.

Add Finishing Touches:

1. Remove the pizza from the oven and let it cool slightly.
2. Sprinkle the chopped cilantro over the pizza for a fresh burst of flavor.
3. Serve with lime wedges on the side for extra zing, and sprinkle additional chili powder or Tajín if desired.

Serve: Slice and serve immediately. Pair with a chilled margarita or an ice-cold Mexican lager for the ultimate street-food-inspired experience.

Nutritional Information (Per Serving)

- **Calories**: 400
- **Protein**: 14g
- **Fat**: 18g
- **Saturated Fat**: 7g
- **Carbohydrates**: 45g
- **Fiber**: 3g
- **Sugar**: 4g
- **Sodium**: 620mg

This Mexican Street Corn Pizza is inspired by my favorite summer treat: elote, a grilled Mexican street corn slathered in crema, lime, and spices. The first time I tried elote, I was at a lively food truck festival, and the combination of smoky corn, tangy lime, and creamy cheese was unforgettable. I wanted to capture that magic in a new way, and pizza felt like the perfect canvas.

The first time I served this pizza was at a backyard barbecue. As the tangy lime crema mingled with the sweet, roasted corn and the slight heat of the jalapeños, my friends couldn't stop raving. It quickly became a crowd favorite, combining the flavors of a street food classic with the indulgence of pizza.

What I love most about this pizza is how it brings people together—it's vibrant, flavorful, and feels like a celebration with every bite. Whether it's a casual weeknight dinner or a summer party, this pizza always steals the show.

Notes

- *Corn Variations*: If fresh corn isn't available, canned or frozen corn works perfectly. Just be sure to char it slightly for added flavor.
- *Cheese Options*: Substitute Cotija with feta for a similar tangy, crumbly texture if Cotija isn't available.
- *Extra Heat*: Add thin slices of serrano peppers or a drizzle of hot sauce for those who enjoy a spicier kick.
- *Serving Tip*: For a more portable option, create personal-sized pizzas or flatbreads using this recipe.

Greek Spanakopita Pizza

Serving Size: 4 servings
Prep Time: 25 minutes
Cook Time: 15-18 minutes
Total Time: 40-45 minutes

Ingredients
For the Crust:

- 1 pizza dough (store-bought or homemade)
- 2 tablespoons unsalted butter, melted
- 1/4 cup plain breadcrumbs

For the Spinach Filling:

- 2 tablespoons olive oil
- 2 cloves garlic, minced
- 1/2 red onion, thinly sliced
- 4 cups fresh spinach, chopped (or 10 ounces frozen, thawed and drained)
- 1/2 teaspoon salt
- 1/4 teaspoon black pepper
- 1 teaspoon dried oregano
- 1 tablespoon fresh dill, chopped (or 1 teaspoon dried)
- 1/2 cup ricotta cheese
- 1/2 cup crumbled feta cheese

For Toppings:

- 1/2 cup shredded mozzarella cheese
- 1/4 cup additional feta, crumbled
- 1 tablespoon olive oil, for brushing
- 1 teaspoon sesame seeds (optional)

For Serving:

- Tzatziki sauce (store-bought or homemade)
- Lemon wedges

Instructions
Prepare the Spinach Filling:

1. Heat olive oil in a skillet over medium heat. Add garlic and sliced red onion, sautéing until fragrant and softened (about 3 minutes).
2. Add the chopped spinach, salt, black pepper, and oregano. Sauté until the spinach is wilted and most of the moisture has evaporated (about 5 minutes).
3. Remove from heat and stir in the fresh dill, ricotta cheese, and crumbled feta. Set aside to cool slightly.

Prepare the Crust:

1. Preheat your oven to 475°F (245°C) and place a pizza stone or baking sheet inside to heat.
2. Roll out the pizza dough on a floured surface to your desired thickness.
3. Brush the surface of the dough with melted butter and sprinkle an even layer of breadcrumbs over the top, pressing gently so they adhere.

Assemble the Pizza:

1. Transfer the prepared dough to a piece of parchment paper.
2. Spread the spinach and ricotta mixture evenly over the dough, leaving a small border around the edges.
3. Sprinkle with shredded mozzarella and additional

crumbled feta.

4. Brush the crust edges with olive oil and sprinkle with sesame seeds for added texture.

Bake the Pizza:

1. Carefully transfer the pizza (with parchment paper) onto the preheated stone or baking sheet.
2. Bake for 15-18 minutes, or until the crust is golden brown and crisp, and the cheese is melted and bubbly.

Serve:

1. Remove the pizza from the oven and let it cool slightly.
2. Serve with a side of tzatziki sauce and lemon wedges for an extra burst of freshness.
3. Slice and enjoy!

Nutritional Information (Per Serving)

- **Calories**: 390
- **Protein**: 15g
- **Fat**: 18g
- **Saturated Fat**: 9g
- **Carbohydrates**: 42g
- **Fiber**: 3g
- **Sugar**: 3g
- **Sodium**: 620mg

Spanakopita has always been one of my favorite Greek dishes. The first time I tried it, I was sitting in a small, family-run taverna in Santorini, where the flaky phyllo layers, warm feta, and bright herbs stole my heart. I wanted to bring that experience home, but with a fun twist—so, naturally, I turned it into a pizza!

The first time I made this, I worried that a pizza crust wouldn't replicate the crisp, buttery layers of phyllo. But with the clever addition of butter and breadcrumbs, the crust develops a delicate crunch that mimics that classic texture. When I served it at a gathering, my friends were instantly transported to the Mediterranean, and it became an instant hit.

What I love most about this recipe is its balance—earthy spinach, creamy ricotta, tangy feta, and warm spices come together beautifully. Plus, dipping each bite into tzatziki just elevates it even more. Every time I make this pizza, I'm reminded of the sun-drenched terraces of Greece and the joy of sharing food that tells a story.

Notes

- *Make It Extra Crispy*: Brush the entire crust with butter before baking for even more flakiness.
- *Cheese Variations*: Swap feta for goat cheese if you prefer a milder, creamier texture.
- *Topping Additions*: Add sliced kalamata olives or sun-dried tomatoes for a more traditional Greek flavor.
- *Meal Pairing*: Serve with a simple Greek salad and a glass of chilled white wine for a complete Mediterranean-inspired meal.

Indian Butter Chicken Pizza

Serving Size: 4 servings
Prep Time: 25 minutes
Cook Time: 15-18 minutes
Total Time: 40-45 minutes

Ingredients
For the Butter Chicken:

- 1 boneless, skinless chicken breast, cut into bite-sized pieces
- 1/2 cup plain yogurt
- 1 tablespoon lemon juice
- 1 teaspoon garam masala
- 1 teaspoon ground cumin
- 1/2 teaspoon ground coriander
- 1/2 teaspoon paprika
- 1/2 teaspoon turmeric
- 1/2 teaspoon salt
- 1 tablespoon butter (for cooking)

For the Butter Chicken Sauce:

- 1 tablespoon butter
- 1/2 cup tomato puree
- 1/2 cup heavy cream
- 2 garlic cloves, minced
- 1 teaspoon grated ginger
- 1 teaspoon garam masala
- 1 teaspoon ground cumin
- 1/2 teaspoon chili powder (adjust to taste)
- Salt to taste

For the Pizza Base:

- 2 naan breads (or 1 large pizza dough, rolled out)
- 1 tablespoon melted butter
- 1 teaspoon minced garlic

For the Toppings:

- 1 1/2 cups shredded mozzarella cheese
- 1/2 small red onion, thinly sliced
- 1/4 cup fresh cilantro, chopped

Optional Garnish:

- Drizzle of plain yogurt or mint chutney
- Crushed red pepper flakes (for extra spice)

Instructions

Prepare the Butter Chicken:

1. In a bowl, mix yogurt, lemon juice, garam masala, cumin, coriander, paprika, turmeric, and salt.
2. Add the chicken pieces and toss to coat. Let it marinate for at least 15 minutes (or up to 2 hours for deeper flavor).
3. Heat a pan over medium-high heat and melt 1 tablespoon of butter. Cook the marinated chicken for about 6-8 minutes, stirring occasionally, until fully cooked. Remove from heat and set aside.

Make the Butter Chicken Sauce:

1. In the same pan, melt 1 tablespoon of butter over medium heat. Add minced garlic and grated ginger, sautéing for 1 minute until fragrant.
2. Stir in the tomato puree, garam masala, cumin, chili

powder, and salt. Simmer for 5 minutes, stirring occasionally.

3. Pour in the heavy cream, stirring until the sauce is smooth and slightly thickened. Simmer for another 2-3 minutes.
4. Add the cooked chicken back into the sauce, coating it evenly. Remove from heat.

Prepare the Pizza Base:

1. Preheat your oven to 475°F (245°C) and place a pizza stone or baking sheet inside to heat.
2. If using naan, brush each piece lightly with melted butter and sprinkle with minced garlic for extra flavor. If using pizza dough, roll it out and follow the same step.

Assemble the Pizza:

1. Spread a generous layer of the butter chicken sauce over the naan or pizza dough.
2. Sprinkle shredded mozzarella evenly on top.
3. Distribute the butter chicken pieces across the pizza.
4. Scatter thinly sliced red onion over the toppings.

Bake the Pizza:

1. Carefully transfer the pizza onto the preheated stone or baking sheet.
2. Bake for 12-15 minutes, or until the crust is golden and the cheese is melted and bubbly.

Add Finishing Touches:

1. Remove from the oven and let the pizza cool slightly.
2. Sprinkle fresh cilantro over the pizza.

3. Drizzle with plain yogurt or mint chutney for a refreshing contrast.

4. Slice and serve immediately.

Nutritional Information (Per Serving)

- **Calories**: 480
- **Protein**: 28g
- **Fat**: 22g
- **Saturated Fat**: 11g
- **Carbohydrates**: 45g
- **Fiber**: 3g
- **Sugar**: 5g
- **Sodium**: 780mg

I first fell in love with butter chicken at a tiny, family-run Indian restaurant where the aroma of warm spices filled the air. It was a dish that felt like a hug—rich, creamy, and full of deep flavors. Years later, I found myself experimenting in my own kitchen, trying to recreate those comforting flavors in new ways.

The idea for this Butter Chicken Pizza came one evening when I had leftover curry but no rice. Looking for an alternative, I spread the buttery sauce onto some naan, topped it with cheese, and baked it into a pizza. The result was pure magic—the fusion of Indian and Italian flavors was unexpectedly perfect.

This dish has since become a go-to for family dinners, and every time I serve it, I watch people light up with excitement at the first bite. It's proof that some of the best recipes come from happy accidents!

Notes

- *Naan vs. Pizza Dough*: Naan provides a softer, chewier

texture, while traditional pizza dough creates a crispier base. Both work wonderfully!

- *Cheese Alternatives*: Swap mozzarella for a blend of mozzarella and Monterey Jack for extra meltiness.
- *Extra Spice*: Add a pinch of red pepper flakes to the sauce or drizzle with extra chili oil before serving.
- *Pairing Suggestion*: Serve with a simple cucumber raita or a refreshing mango lassi to balance the richness of the butter chicken.

Japanese Teriyaki Salmon Pizza

Serving Size: 4 servings

Prep Time: 25 minutes

Cook Time: 12-15 minutes

Total Time: 40 minutes

Ingredients

For the Teriyaki Salmon:

- 1 salmon fillet (about 6 ounces), skin removed
- 1/4 cup soy sauce
- 2 tablespoons mirin
- 2 tablespoons honey or brown sugar
- 1 tablespoon rice vinegar
- 1 teaspoon grated ginger
- 1 teaspoon sesame oil
- 1 teaspoon cornstarch (optional, for thickening)

For the Teriyaki Glaze (Pizza Sauce):

- 1/4 cup reserved teriyaki marinade (from above)
- 1 teaspoon sesame oil
- 1 teaspoon cornstarch + 2 teaspoons water (slurry, optional)

For the Pizza Base:

- 1 pizza dough (store-bought or homemade)
- 1 tablespoon olive oil or sesame oil

For the Toppings:

- 1 1/2 cups shredded mozzarella cheese

- 1/2 cup julienned carrots
- 1/2 cup snow peas, sliced thinly
- 2 scallions, sliced diagonally
- 1 tablespoon toasted sesame seeds

For Garnish:

- 1 sheet shredded nori (dried seaweed)
- Extra teriyaki glaze for drizzling (optional)
- Pickled ginger (optional, for serving)

Instructions
Prepare the Teriyaki Salmon:

1. In a small bowl, mix soy sauce, mirin, honey (or brown sugar), rice vinegar, grated ginger, and sesame oil.
2. Place the salmon fillet in a shallow dish and pour the marinade over it. Let it marinate for at least 15 minutes.
3. Heat a skillet over medium-high heat. Remove salmon from the marinade (reserving 1/4 cup for the glaze) and sear for 2-3 minutes per side until cooked through. Remove from heat and shred into bite-sized pieces.

Make the Teriyaki Glaze (Pizza Sauce):

1. In a small saucepan, heat the reserved teriyaki marinade with sesame oil over medium heat.
2. If a thicker sauce is desired, add the cornstarch slurry and whisk until the sauce thickens slightly. Remove from heat and let cool.

Prepare the Pizza Base:

1. Preheat your oven to 475°F (245°C) and place a pizza

stone or baking sheet inside to heat.

2. Roll out the pizza dough on a floured surface to your desired thickness.
3. Transfer the dough to a parchment-lined surface, brush lightly with olive or sesame oil, and spread an even layer of teriyaki glaze over the surface, leaving a small border around the edges.

Assemble the Pizza:

1. Sprinkle shredded mozzarella cheese evenly over the sauce.
2. Distribute the shredded teriyaki salmon across the pizza.
3. Add the julienned carrots and snow peas.

Bake the Pizza:

1. Carefully transfer the pizza (with parchment paper) onto the preheated stone or baking sheet.
2. Bake for 12-15 minutes, or until the crust is golden and the cheese is melted and bubbly.

Add Finishing Touches:

1. Remove the pizza from the oven and let it cool slightly.
2. Sprinkle sliced scallions and toasted sesame seeds over the top.
3. Garnish with shredded nori and drizzle with extra teriyaki glaze if desired.

Serve: Slice and serve immediately. For an authentic Japanese touch, serve with a side of pickled ginger and a drizzle of wasabi mayo for extra heat.

Nutritional Information (Per Serving)

- **Calories**: 420
- **Protein**: 25g
- **Fat**: 14g
- **Saturated Fat**: 5g
- **Carbohydrates**: 45g
- **Fiber**: 3g
- **Sugar**: 10g
- **Sodium**: 850mg

The inspiration for this Japanese Teriyaki Salmon Pizza came from a sushi-making night gone wrong—well, sort of! I had planned a sushi dinner, but my homemade sushi rolls didn't hold together quite right. Not wanting to waste the ingredients, I decided to turn the components into a pizza instead. What started as a quick experiment turned into one of the best fusion dishes I've ever made!

The balance of flavors is what makes this pizza stand out. The sweet and savory teriyaki sauce caramelizes beautifully in the oven, while the crispy snow peas and carrots add a fresh crunch. Topping it with nori enhances the umami flavor, making it taste just like a deconstructed sushi roll—but with the satisfaction of a warm, melty pizza.

Now, this dish has become a staple in my home whenever I want something unique yet comforting. It's a fantastic way to introduce sushi lovers to a new take on their favorite flavors!

Notes

- *Crust Variation*: For an extra crispy, sushi-style experience, use a thin flatbread like lavash instead of traditional pizza dough.
- *Cheese Alternative*: Swap mozzarella for Monterey Jack or skip the cheese altogether for a more traditional Japanese flavor.

- *Extra Crunch*: Sprinkle with crispy fried onions or tempura flakes for added texture.
- *Serving Suggestion*: Pair with a glass of chilled sake or a light Japanese beer like Asahi for the ultimate experience.

Moroccan Vegetable Tagine Pizza

Serving Size: 4 servings
Prep Time: 30 minutes
Cook Time: 12-15 minutes
Total Time: 45 minutes

Ingredients
For the Spiced Tomato & Harissa Sauce:

- 1 tablespoon olive oil
- 1 small onion, finely chopped
- 2 cloves garlic, minced
- 1 teaspoon ground cumin
- 1 teaspoon ground coriander
- 1/2 teaspoon ground cinnamon
- 1/2 teaspoon smoked paprika
- 1/2 teaspoon ground turmeric
- 1 tablespoon harissa paste (adjust to taste)
- 1 cup canned crushed tomatoes
- 1 teaspoon honey or maple syrup (optional, for balance)
- Salt and black pepper to taste

For the Roasted Vegetables:

- 1 small eggplant, diced
- 1 small zucchini, diced
- 1/2 cup canned chickpeas, drained and rinsed
- 1 tablespoon olive oil
- 1/2 teaspoon salt
- 1/2 teaspoon ground cumin
- 1/4 teaspoon black pepper

For the Pizza Base:

- 1 pizza dough (store-bought or homemade)
- 1 tablespoon olive oil

For the Toppings:

- 1/4 cup chopped preserved lemons (rinsed to reduce saltiness)
- 1/2 cup crumbled plant-based feta (or regular feta if not vegan)
- 1/4 teaspoon red pepper flakes (optional, for heat)

For Garnish:

- 2 tablespoons fresh mint leaves, chopped
- 2 tablespoons pomegranate seeds
- Drizzle of extra harissa or olive oil

Instructions

Prepare the Spiced Tomato & Harissa Sauce:

1. Heat olive oil in a saucepan over medium heat. Add chopped onion and sauté for 3-4 minutes until softened.
2. Stir in garlic, cumin, coriander, cinnamon, smoked paprika, and turmeric, cooking for another minute until fragrant.
3. Add harissa paste and crushed tomatoes, stirring to combine. Simmer for 5-7 minutes, allowing the flavors to meld.
4. Taste and adjust seasoning with salt, pepper, and honey/ maple syrup if desired. Remove from heat and set aside.

Roast the Vegetables:

1. Preheat your oven to 400°F (200°C).
2. In a bowl, toss diced eggplant, zucchini, and chickpeas with olive oil, salt, cumin, and black pepper.
3. Spread on a baking sheet in a single layer and roast for 15-20 minutes, or until golden and tender. Remove from the oven and set aside.

Prepare the Pizza Base:

1. Increase the oven temperature to 475°F (245°C) and place a pizza stone or baking sheet inside to heat.
2. Roll out the pizza dough on a floured surface to your desired thickness.
3. Brush the dough lightly with olive oil.

Assemble the Pizza:

1. Spread an even layer of the spiced tomato & harissa sauce over the dough, leaving a small border around the edges.
2. Evenly distribute the roasted eggplant, zucchini, and chickpeas.
3. Scatter chopped preserved lemons and crumbled plant-based feta across the top.
4. Sprinkle with red pepper flakes if desired.

Bake the Pizza:

1. Carefully transfer the pizza (with parchment paper) onto the preheated stone or baking sheet.
2. Bake for 12-15 minutes, or until the crust is golden and the toppings are slightly caramelized.

Add Finishing Touches:

1. Remove from the oven and let it cool slightly.
2. Sprinkle with fresh mint and pomegranate seeds.
3. Drizzle with extra harissa or olive oil for added richness.

Serve: Slice and serve immediately. Enjoy with a side of warm couscous salad or a refreshing glass of mint tea.

Nutritional Information (Per Serving)

- **Calories**: 390
- **Protein**: 12g
- **Fat**: 14g
- **Saturated Fat**: 3g
- **Carbohydrates**: 55g
- **Fiber**: 8g
- **Sugar**: 9g
- **Sodium**: 720mg

I was introduced to Moroccan cuisine at a small family-run restaurant where I had my first taste of a traditional vegetable tagine. The combination of warm spices, slow-cooked vegetables, and preserved lemons was unlike anything I had ever experienced. I remember savoring every bite, fascinated by the layers of flavor—sweet, smoky, tangy, and deeply aromatic.

Years later, I decided to bring those flavors into a new format, and this pizza was born. The harissa-spiced tomato sauce provides a bold foundation, while the roasted vegetables soak up the warm spices. The preserved lemons add that unmistakable Moroccan tang, and the fresh mint and pomegranate seeds give it a final, refreshing lift.

This recipe is a celebration of Moroccan flavors in a fun and modern way. Every time I make it, I'm reminded of that first unforgettable meal and the joy of experimenting with global flavors in my own kitchen.

Notes

- *Preserved Lemons Alternative*: If you can't find preserved lemons, substitute with a mix of lemon zest and a touch of salt.
- *Extra Protein*: Add spiced lentils or crumbled tempeh for an extra protein boost.
- *Cheese Options*: Use dairy feta if not making a vegan version.
- *Make It Gluten-Free*: Use a gluten-free pizza crust to accommodate dietary preferences.

Thai Peanut Chicken Pizza

Serving Size: 4 servings
Prep Time: 25 minutes
Cook Time: 12-15 minutes
Total Time: 40 minutes

Ingredients

For the Thai Peanut Sauce (Pizza Base):

- 1/4 cup creamy peanut butter
- 2 tablespoons soy sauce
- 1 tablespoon hoisin sauce
- 1 tablespoon rice vinegar
- 1 tablespoon lime juice
- 1 teaspoon grated ginger
- 1 teaspoon sriracha (adjust to taste)
- 1 teaspoon honey (optional)
- 2 tablespoons warm water (to thin)

For the Grilled Chicken:

- 1 boneless, skinless chicken breast
- 1 tablespoon soy sauce
- 1 teaspoon sesame oil
- 1 teaspoon lime juice
- 1/2 teaspoon garlic powder
- 1/4 teaspoon black pepper

For the Pizza Base:

- 1 pizza dough (store-bought or homemade)
- 1 tablespoon olive oil

For the Toppings:

- 1 1/2 cups shredded mozzarella cheese
- 1/2 cup shredded carrots
- 1/2 red bell pepper, thinly sliced
- 1/4 cup crushed peanuts
- 2 tablespoons fresh cilantro, chopped

For Garnish:

- Lime wedges
- Extra sriracha for drizzling

Instructions

Prepare the Thai Peanut Sauce:

1. In a bowl, whisk together peanut butter, soy sauce, hoisin sauce, rice vinegar, lime juice, grated ginger, sriracha, and honey (if using).
2. Add warm water gradually to thin out the sauce until smooth and spreadable. Set aside.

Cook the Grilled Chicken:

1. In a small bowl, mix soy sauce, sesame oil, lime juice, garlic powder, and black pepper.
2. Coat the chicken in the marinade and let sit for at least 10 minutes.
3. Heat a grill pan over medium-high heat and cook the chicken for about 4-5 minutes per side until fully cooked.
4. Remove from heat, let it rest for a few minutes, then slice into thin strips.

Prepare the Pizza Base:

1. Preheat your oven to 475°F (245°C) and place a pizza stone or baking sheet inside to heat.
2. Roll out the pizza dough on a floured surface to your desired thickness.
3. Transfer the dough to a parchment-lined surface and brush lightly with olive oil.

Assemble the Pizza:

1. Spread an even layer of the Thai peanut sauce over the dough, leaving a small border around the edges.
2. Sprinkle shredded mozzarella cheese evenly over the sauce.
3. Distribute the grilled chicken slices, shredded carrots, and red bell pepper slices over the cheese.

Bake the Pizza:

1. Carefully transfer the pizza (with parchment paper) onto the preheated stone or baking sheet.
2. Bake for 12-15 minutes, or until the crust is golden and the cheese is melted and bubbly.

Add Finishing Touches:

1. Remove the pizza from the oven and let it cool slightly.
2. Sprinkle crushed peanuts and fresh cilantro over the top.
3. Serve with lime wedges and drizzle with extra sriracha for a spicy kick.

Serve: Slice and serve immediately. Pair with a cold Thai iced tea or a light coconut water for a refreshing contrast.

Nutritional Information (Per Serving)

- **Calories**: 450

- **Protein**: 27g
- **Fat**: 20g
- **Saturated Fat**: 6g
- **Carbohydrates**: 45g
- **Fiber**: 4g
- **Sugar**: 8g
- **Sodium**: 850mg

The first time I had Thai peanut sauce, it was drizzled over a plate of warm noodles at a street food stall in Bangkok. The blend of creamy peanut butter, soy, and lime was unlike anything I had ever tasted—sweet, salty, nutty, and spicy all at once. I instantly fell in love with its bold flavors.

Years later, I wanted to bring that experience into my own kitchen, and I thought, "Why not put it on pizza?" That's how this Thai Peanut Chicken Pizza was born. The grilled chicken absorbs the savory marinade, while the peanut sauce acts as a rich, flavorful base. The fresh carrots and red peppers provide the perfect crunch, and the lime juice ties everything together.

The first time I served this pizza, my friends were skeptical—but after one bite, they were hooked. Now, it's a staple for Thai food lovers and pizza fans alike!

Notes

- *Spice Level*: Adjust the heat by adding more or less sriracha in the peanut sauce.
- *Peanut-Free Alternative*: Substitute almond or sunflower butter for a nut-free option.
- *Extra Crunch*: Garnish with crispy shallots or fried wonton strips.
- *Vegetarian Option*: Swap chicken for tofu or roasted mushrooms for a plant-based version.

- *Pairing Idea*: Serve with a Thai mango salad or a coconut soup for a complete meal.

Caribbean Jerk Shrimp Pizza

Serving Size: 4 servings
Prep Time: 25 minutes
Cook Time: 12-15 minutes
Total Time: 40 minutes

Ingredients
For the Jerk-Seasoned Shrimp:

- 8 ounces large shrimp, peeled and deveined
- 1 tablespoon olive oil
- 1 teaspoon jerk seasoning (store-bought or homemade)
- 1/2 teaspoon smoked paprika
- 1/2 teaspoon garlic powder
- 1/2 teaspoon thyme
- 1/4 teaspoon cayenne pepper (optional, for extra heat)
- 1 teaspoon lime juice

For the Jerk-Spiced Tomato Sauce:

- 1/2 cup canned crushed tomatoes
- 1 tablespoon tomato paste
- 1 teaspoon jerk seasoning
- 1 teaspoon honey
- 1 teaspoon lime juice
- 1 teaspoon olive oil
- 1/4 teaspoon black pepper

For the Pizza Base:

- 1 pizza dough (store-bought or homemade)
- 1 tablespoon olive oil

For the Toppings:

- 1 1/2 cups shredded mozzarella cheese
- 1/2 cup fresh pineapple chunks
- 1/2 small red onion, thinly sliced
- 1/2 red bell pepper, sliced thinly
- 1/2 teaspoon red pepper flakes (optional, for heat)

For Garnish:

- 2 tablespoons fresh parsley or cilantro, chopped
- Extra lime wedges for serving

Instructions
Prepare the Jerk Shrimp:

1. In a bowl, toss the shrimp with olive oil, jerk seasoning, smoked paprika, garlic powder, thyme, cayenne pepper (if using), and lime juice. Let marinate for at least 15 minutes.
2. Heat a skillet over medium-high heat and cook the shrimp for 2-3 minutes per side until opaque and slightly charred. Remove from heat and set aside.

Make the Jerk-Spiced Tomato Sauce:

1. In a small saucepan, heat olive oil over medium heat.
2. Add crushed tomatoes, tomato paste, jerk seasoning, honey, lime juice, and black pepper. Stir and let simmer for 5 minutes until slightly thickened. Set aside to cool.

Prepare the Pizza Base:

1. Preheat your oven to 475°F (245°C) and place a pizza stone or baking sheet inside to heat.
2. Roll out the pizza dough on a floured surface to your

desired thickness.

3. Transfer the dough to a parchment-lined surface and brush
   lightly with olive oil.

Assemble the Pizza:

1. Spread an even layer of the jerk-spiced tomato sauce over
   the dough, leaving a small border around the edges.
2. Sprinkle shredded mozzarella cheese evenly over the sauce.
3. Distribute the cooked jerk shrimp, pineapple chunks, red
   onion, and red bell pepper over the pizza.
4. Sprinkle with red pepper flakes for extra heat, if desired.

Bake the Pizza:

1. Carefully transfer the pizza (with parchment paper) onto
   the preheated stone or baking sheet.
2. Bake for 12-15 minutes, or until the crust is golden and the
   cheese is melted and bubbly.

Add Finishing Touches:

1. Remove the pizza from the oven and let it cool slightly.
2. Sprinkle with chopped fresh parsley or cilantro for a burst
   of freshness.
3. Serve with lime wedges for extra zing.

Serve: Slice and enjoy immediately with a cold rum punch or a
tropical smoothie for the ultimate island experience.

Nutritional Information (Per Serving)

- **Calories**: 450
- **Protein**: 28g
- **Fat**: 14g

- **Saturated Fat**: 6g
- **Carbohydrates**: 52g
- **Fiber**: 3g
- **Sugar**: 9g
- **Sodium**: 850mg

This Caribbean Jerk Shrimp Pizza was inspired by a trip to Jamaica, where I first experienced the vibrant, smoky flavors of jerk seasoning. I still remember the aroma of jerk chicken grilling on open flames, paired with the sweetness of grilled pineapple and the cool ocean breeze. It was an unforgettable combination of spice, sweetness, and freshness.

Years later, I wanted to bring those flavors into my own kitchen, but with a creative twist—so I put them on a pizza! The result was a perfect balance of heat from the jerk shrimp, sweetness from the pineapple, and freshness from the herbs. The moment I served it to friends, it was a hit, instantly transporting us to the tropics with every bite.

Now, this pizza is my go-to when I want a fun and bold meal, and it always sparks conversation about travel, food, and warm island memories.

Notes

- *Jerk Seasoning Alternative*: If you can't find pre-made jerk seasoning, mix equal parts allspice, garlic powder, smoked paprika, thyme, cinnamon, and cayenne.
- *Pineapple Lovers*: Try grilling the pineapple chunks before adding them to the pizza for a caramelized, smoky sweetness.
- *Extra Kick*: Drizzle with a scotch bonnet pepper sauce for an authentic Jamaican spice.
- *Serving Pairing*: Enjoy with coconut rice or a mango slaw

for a full Caribbean-inspired meal.

191

French Ratatouille Pizza

Serving Size: 4 servings
Prep Time: 30 minutes
Cook Time: 12-15 minutes
Total Time: 45 minutes

Ingredients
For the Garlic-Infused Olive Oil (Pizza Base Sauce):

- 3 tablespoons extra virgin olive oil
- 2 cloves garlic, minced
- 1 teaspoon herbes de Provence
- 1/2 teaspoon salt
- 1/4 teaspoon black pepper

For the Roasted Ratatouille Vegetables:

- 1/2 small eggplant, thinly sliced
- 1/2 small zucchini, thinly sliced
- 1/2 red bell pepper, thinly sliced
- 1/2 cup cherry tomatoes, halved
- 1 tablespoon olive oil
- 1/2 teaspoon salt
- 1/4 teaspoon black pepper
- 1 teaspoon herbes de Provence

For the Pizza Base:

- 1 pizza dough (store-bought or homemade)
- 1 tablespoon olive oil

For the Toppings:

- 1 cup shredded mozzarella cheese
- 1/4 cup crumbled goat cheese
- 1 teaspoon red pepper flakes (optional, for a slight kick)
- 1 tablespoon balsamic glaze (for drizzling)

For Garnish:

- 2 tablespoons fresh basil or parsley, chopped
- Extra herbes de Provence (for sprinkling)

Instructions

Prepare the Garlic-Infused Olive Oil:

1. In a small saucepan, heat olive oil over low heat.
2. Add minced garlic and herbes de Provence, cooking for 1-2 minutes until fragrant but not browned.
3. Remove from heat, stir in salt and black pepper, and set aside.

Roast the Ratatouille Vegetables:

1. Preheat oven to 400°F (200°C).
2. In a mixing bowl, toss the eggplant, zucchini, red bell pepper, and cherry tomatoes with olive oil, salt, black pepper, and herbes de Provence.
3. Spread the vegetables in a single layer on a baking sheet and roast for 15-18 minutes until tender and slightly caramelized. Remove from the oven and set aside.

Prepare the Pizza Base:

1. Increase oven temperature to 475°F (245°C) and place a pizza stone or baking sheet inside to heat.
2. Roll out the pizza dough on a floured surface to your

desired thickness.

3. Transfer the dough to a parchment-lined surface and brush lightly with the prepared garlic-infused olive oil.

Assemble the Pizza:

1. Sprinkle shredded mozzarella evenly over the garlic-infused dough.
2. Arrange the roasted ratatouille vegetables in an overlapping pattern on top of the cheese.
3. Scatter crumbled goat cheese across the pizza.
4. Sprinkle with red pepper flakes if using.

Bake the Pizza:

1. Carefully transfer the pizza (with parchment paper) onto the preheated stone or baking sheet.
2. Bake for 12-15 minutes, or until the crust is golden and the cheese is melted and bubbly.

Add Finishing Touches:

1. Remove from the oven and let the pizza cool slightly.
2. Drizzle with balsamic glaze for a hint of sweetness and tang.
3. Sprinkle fresh basil or parsley over the top for added brightness.
4. Serve immediately.

Nutritional Information (Per Serving)

- **Calories**: 420
- **Protein**: 15g
- **Fat**: 18g

- **Saturated Fat**: 7g
- **Carbohydrates**: 50g
- **Fiber**: 5g
- **Sugar**: 7g
- **Sodium**: 600mg

I first fell in love with ratatouille during a visit to Provence, where I tasted a slow-cooked version at a charming countryside café. The way the flavors of zucchini, eggplant, and tomatoes blended together was mesmerizing. The freshness of the herbs, the richness of the olive oil, and the hint of sweetness from the tomatoes made it a dish that stayed with me long after the trip ended.

Bringing those flavors to a pizza felt like the perfect fusion of French rustic cuisine and the comfort of Italian tradition. The garlic-infused olive oil base keeps things light while enhancing the natural sweetness of the roasted vegetables. And when I served this for the first time, the balsamic glaze added the final touch, making each bite feel like a taste of Provence.

This French Ratatouille Pizza is my way of bringing the warmth and elegance of the French countryside into a dish that's perfect for sharing.

Notes

- *Cheese Alternatives*: Swap goat cheese for feta or a sprinkle of Parmesan for a different flavor profile.
- *Extra Crisp Crust*: Pre-bake the crust for 5 minutes before adding toppings to get an extra crispy texture.
- *Serving Suggestion*: Pair with a glass of chilled Sauvignon Blanc or a classic French rosé.
- *Make It Gluten-Free*: Use a gluten-free pizza dough to accommodate dietary needs.

Hawaiian Poke Pizza

Serving Size: 4 servings
Prep Time: 25 minutes
Cook Time: 10-12 minutes
Total Time: 35 minutes

Ingredients

For the Soy-Ginger Glaze (Pizza Base Sauce):

- 1/4 cup soy sauce
- 1 tablespoon honey or maple syrup
- 1 tablespoon rice vinegar
- 1 teaspoon grated ginger
- 1 teaspoon sesame oil
- 1 teaspoon cornstarch + 2 teaspoons water (slurry, optional for thickening)

For the Poke Topping:

- 6 ounces sushi-grade ahi tuna, diced
- 1 teaspoon soy sauce
- 1 teaspoon sesame oil
- 1 teaspoon rice vinegar
- 1/2 teaspoon grated ginger
- 1/2 teaspoon sriracha (optional, for heat)

For the Pizza Base:

- 1 thin pizza crust (pre-baked flatbread, naan, or a crispy thin-crust dough)
- 1 tablespoon olive oil

For the Toppings:

- 1/2 cup shredded mozzarella cheese (optional, for a fusion twist)
- 1/2 avocado, diced
- 1/2 cup cucumber, thinly sliced
- 2 tablespoons pickled ginger, chopped
- 1 tablespoon sesame seeds (white or black)
- 1 scallion, finely sliced

For Garnish:

- 1 sheet shredded nori (dried seaweed)
- Extra drizzle of soy-ginger glaze
- Microgreens or fresh cilantro (optional)

Instructions

Prepare the Soy-Ginger Glaze:

1. In a small saucepan over medium heat, combine soy sauce, honey, rice vinegar, grated ginger, and sesame oil.
2. If thickening the glaze, mix cornstarch with water to create a slurry, then whisk it into the sauce.
3. Simmer for 2-3 minutes until slightly thickened. Remove from heat and let cool.

Prepare the Poke Tuna:

1. In a small bowl, combine diced ahi tuna with soy sauce, sesame oil, rice vinegar, grated ginger, and sriracha (if using).
2. Gently toss to coat and refrigerate for at least 10 minutes while preparing the pizza.

Prepare the Pizza Base:

1. Preheat oven to 400°F (200°C).
2. Brush the pre-baked flatbread or pizza crust with olive oil.
3. Lightly toast in the oven for 5-7 minutes until crisp. If using shredded mozzarella, add it before baking for a fusion-style warm base.

Assemble the Pizza:

1. Once the crust is slightly cooled, spread a thin layer of the soy-ginger glaze over the surface.
2. Evenly distribute the marinated ahi tuna over the pizza.
3. Scatter diced avocado, sliced cucumber, and chopped pickled ginger across the top.
4. Sprinkle with sesame seeds and sliced scallions.

Add Finishing Touches:

1. Garnish with shredded nori for an umami boost.
2. Drizzle extra soy-ginger glaze over the pizza.
3. For a fresh contrast, top with microgreens or cilantro.

Serve: Slice and serve chilled or at room temperature for a sushi-inspired experience. Pair with a cold glass of sake or a tropical fruit-infused sparkling water for a refreshing complement.

Nutritional Information (Per Serving)

- **Calories**: 380
- **Protein**: 24g
- **Fat**: 15g
- **Saturated Fat**: 3g
- **Carbohydrates**: 38g
- **Fiber**: 4g
- **Sugar**: 6g

- **Sodium**: 850mg

This Hawaiian Poke Pizza was inspired by a trip to Oahu, where I had my first taste of authentic poke. The freshness of the marinated tuna, the creamy avocado, and the crunch of cucumbers created an unforgettable bite. I wanted to capture those flavors in a fun, unexpected way, and pizza felt like the perfect vehicle.

The first time I made this dish, I was skeptical—would raw tuna on pizza really work? But as soon as I took the first bite, I knew I had something special. The soy-ginger glaze added a perfect umami base, and the combination of warm crispy crust with cool, delicate toppings created a stunning contrast. Now, it's a favorite for sushi lovers and adventurous foodies alike!

Notes

- *Raw Tuna Safety*: Always use sushi-grade ahi tuna for this recipe, and keep it refrigerated until serving.
- *Gluten-Free Option*: Use a gluten-free flatbread or cauliflower crust.
- *Vegetarian Alternative*: Substitute marinated tofu or watermelon poke instead of tuna for a plant-based version.
- *Extra Crunch*: Add crispy fried wonton strips or crushed macadamia nuts for added texture.
- *Serving Suggestion*: Pair with chilled sake, a lychee martini, or coconut water for a tropical touch.

World Comfort Pizzas

1. **Italian Carbonara Pizza**: Inspired by the classic Roman pasta dish, this pizza features crispy pancetta, creamy egg yolk sauce, Parmesan, and black pepper for a rich and decadent bite.

2. **American Cheeseburger Pizza**: This pizza brings all the flavors of a juicy, loaded cheeseburger, complete with beef, cheddar, pickles, and a special burger sauce drizzle.

3. **German Pretzel & Beer Cheese Pizza**: A buttery pretzel crust topped with gooey beer cheese, bratwurst slices, and caramelized onions for an Oktoberfest-inspired delight.

4. **Southern BBQ Mac & Cheese Pizza**: A comfort food mashup, this pizza layers creamy mac and cheese, BBQ pulled pork, and a smoky cheddar crust.

5. **British Shepherd's Pie Pizza**: A cozy take on shepherd's pie, this pizza features savory ground lamb, mashed potatoes, and melted cheese for the ultimate hearty bite.

6. **Swedish Meatball Pizza**: Inspired by the famous IKEA Swedish meatballs, this pizza has savory meatballs, lingonberry sauce, and a rich cream sauce base.

7. **Korean Kimchi & Spam Pizza**: A Korean comfort food fusion, this pizza combines crispy Spam, tangy kimchi, melted cheese, and a gochujang cream sauce.

8. **Canadian Poutine Pizza**: A poutine-inspired pizza, topped with crispy fries, cheese curds, and rich brown gravy for the ultimate indulgence.

9. **Argentine Choripán Pizza**: Inspired by Argentina's favorite street food, this pizza features grilled chorizo, chimichurri sauce, and roasted red peppers.

10. **Japanese Okonomiyaki Pizza**: A savory Japanese pancake meets pizza, with shredded cabbage, crispy bacon, and okonomiyaki sauce.

Italian Carbonara Pizza

Serving Size: 4 servings
Prep Time: 20 minutes
Cook Time: 12-15 minutes
Total Time: 35 minutes

Ingredients
For the Garlic Cream Sauce (Pizza Base)

- 1 tablespoon unsalted butter
- 2 cloves garlic, minced
- 3/4 cup heavy cream
- 1/2 cup grated Parmesan cheese
- 1/4 teaspoon salt
- 1/4 teaspoon black pepper

For the Pizza Base

- 1 pizza dough (store-bought or homemade)
- 1 tablespoon olive oil

For the Toppings

- 1 cup shredded mozzarella cheese
- 4 slices pancetta, cooked and crumbled
- 1/2 teaspoon freshly cracked black pepper
- 1/4 cup grated Parmesan cheese
- 2 egg yolks

For Garnish

- 2 tablespoons fresh parsley, chopped

Instructions
Prepare the Garlic Cream Sauce

1. In a saucepan over medium heat, melt the butter and add minced garlic. Sauté for 1 minute.
2. Stir in the heavy cream and bring to a gentle simmer.
3. Add the grated Parmesan, salt, and black pepper, stirring until smooth and slightly thickened. Remove from heat and set aside.

Prepare the Pizza Base

1. Preheat the oven to 475°F (245°C) and place a pizza stone or baking sheet inside to heat.
2. Roll out the pizza dough on a floured surface to your desired thickness.
3. Transfer to a parchment-lined surface and brush with olive oil.

Assemble the Pizza

1. Spread an even layer of the garlic cream sauce over the dough.
2. Sprinkle shredded mozzarella over the sauce.
3. Distribute the crumbled pancetta evenly over the pizza.
4. Sprinkle with freshly cracked black pepper and Parmesan.

Bake the Pizza

1. Transfer the pizza onto the preheated stone or baking sheet.
2. Bake for 12-15 minutes or until the crust is golden and the cheese is bubbly.

Add Finishing Touches

1. Remove from the oven and immediately add the raw egg yolks to the center of the pizza.
2. Sprinkle with fresh parsley and serve immediately.

Nutritional Information (Per Serving)

- **Calories**: 460
- **Protein**: 22g
- **Fat**: 25g
- **Carbohydrates**: 38g
- **Fiber**: 2g
- **Sodium**: 780mg

The first time I had carbonara was in a small Roman trattoria tucked away in a quiet alley, the kind of place where locals gather and conversation flows as easily as the wine. The simplicity of the dish fascinated me—just a handful of ingredients, yet each bite was rich, creamy, and perfectly balanced. I was so inspired by the combination of crispy pancetta, Parmesan, egg yolk, and black pepper that I knew I had to try turning it into a pizza.

When I first made this recipe, I wasn't sure if the delicate creaminess of carbonara would translate well to a crisp pizza crust, but as soon as I took my first bite, I knew it worked. The garlic-infused cream sauce melds beautifully with the melted cheese, while the pancetta adds just the right amount of salt and crunch. The key, of course, is adding the egg yolks after baking, allowing them to gently coat each slice when you cut into it. Now, every time I make this pizza, I'm reminded of that first trip to Rome, of winding cobblestone streets and the comforting warmth of a meal made with love and tradition.

Notes

- Egg yolks should be cracked onto the pizza after baking for an authentic carbonara experience.
- For extra crunch, add crispy fried sage or additional pancetta bits.
- Pairs well with a crisp white wine like Pinot Grigio.

American Cheeseburger Pizza

Serving Size: 4 servings
Prep Time: 20 minutes
Cook Time: 12-15 minutes
Total Time: 35 minutes

Ingredients
For the Special Burger Sauce (Pizza Base)

- 1/4 cup mayonnaise
- 1 tablespoon ketchup
- 1 teaspoon yellow mustard
- 1 teaspoon pickle relish
- 1/2 teaspoon garlic powder
- 1/4 teaspoon paprika

For the Pizza Base

- 1 pizza dough (store-bought or homemade)
- 1 tablespoon olive oil

For the Toppings

- 1 cup shredded cheddar cheese
- 1/2 pound ground beef, cooked and seasoned with salt and pepper
- 1/2 cup dill pickles, sliced
- 1/2 red onion, thinly sliced
- 1/2 cup shredded lettuce (added after baking)

For Garnish

- 2 tablespoons sesame seeds (optional, to mimic a burger

bun)

Instructions
Prepare the Special Burger Sauce

1. In a small bowl, mix together the mayonnaise, ketchup, mustard, pickle relish, garlic powder, and paprika. Stir until smooth and set aside.

Prepare the Pizza Base

1. Preheat the oven to 475°F (245°C) and place a pizza stone or baking sheet inside to heat.
2. Roll out the pizza dough on a floured surface to your desired thickness.
3. Transfer to a parchment-lined surface and brush with olive oil.

Assemble the Pizza

1. Spread an even layer of the special burger sauce over the dough.
2. Sprinkle shredded cheddar cheese over the sauce.
3. Evenly distribute the cooked ground beef across the pizza.
4. Scatter sliced pickles and red onions on top.

Bake the Pizza

1. Transfer the pizza onto the preheated stone or baking sheet.
2. Bake for 12-15 minutes or until the crust is golden and the cheese is bubbly.

Add Finishing Touches

1. Remove from the oven and let cool for 2 minutes.
2. Sprinkle shredded lettuce over the pizza.
3. Optionally, garnish with sesame seeds for a burger bun effect.

Nutritional Information (Per Serving)

- **Calories**: 510
- **Protein**: 28g
- **Fat**: 27g
- **Carbohydrates**: 42g
- **Fiber**: 3g
- **Sodium**: 900mg

One of my favorite childhood memories is going to a local diner with my family for cheeseburgers and fries. There was something about that classic combination of a juicy beef patty, melted cheese, and tangy pickles that always felt like the ultimate comfort food. Years later, I found myself craving those flavors but wanting something a little different—something that combined my love for pizza with the nostalgia of an old-school burger.

This pizza became an instant hit in my kitchen. The special burger sauce gives it that unmistakable fast-food flavor, while the crisp lettuce on top provides a fresh contrast to the melty cheese and seasoned beef. The addition of sesame seeds on the crust was a last-minute experiment, but now I can't make it without them. It's everything you love about a cheeseburger, but in pizza form—and somehow, that makes it even better.

Notes

- Add crispy bacon for a bacon cheeseburger twist.
- For a Big Mac-style pizza, use shredded iceberg lettuce and extra sauce on top after baking.

- Serve with fries on the side for the full burger experience.

German Pretzel & Beer Cheese Pizza

Serving Size: 4 servings
Prep Time: 25 minutes
Cook Time: 12-15 minutes
Total Time: 40 minutes

Ingredients

For the Beer Cheese Sauce (Pizza Base)

- 2 tablespoons unsalted butter
- 2 tablespoons all-purpose flour
- 1/2 cup beer (light lager or German-style beer)
- 1/2 cup whole milk
- 1 teaspoon Dijon mustard
- 1/2 teaspoon garlic powder
- 1 cup shredded sharp cheddar cheese
- Salt and pepper to taste

For the Pretzel Crust

- 1 pizza dough (store-bought or homemade)
- 1 teaspoon baking soda
- 1 tablespoon warm water
- 1 tablespoon coarse sea salt

For the Toppings

- 1/2 cup caramelized onions
- 1/2 cup bratwurst, sliced and pre-cooked
- 1/2 cup shredded mozzarella cheese
- 1/4 cup shredded cheddar cheese

For Garnish

- 1 teaspoon grainy mustard (drizzled after baking)
- 1 tablespoon fresh chopped parsley

Instructions
Prepare the Beer Cheese Sauce

1. In a saucepan over medium heat, melt the butter, then whisk in the flour to create a roux.
2. Slowly pour in the beer and milk, whisking constantly to prevent lumps.
3. Stir in the Dijon mustard and garlic powder.
4. Add shredded cheddar cheese, stirring until fully melted and smooth.
5. Season with salt and pepper to taste. Remove from heat and set aside.

Prepare the Pretzel Crust

1. Preheat the oven to 475°F (245°C) and place a pizza stone or baking sheet inside to heat.
2. Roll out the pizza dough on a floured surface to your desired thickness.
3. In a small bowl, mix the baking soda with warm water, then brush the mixture onto the outer crust of the dough.
4. Sprinkle the outer crust with coarse sea salt for a pretzel-like texture.

Assemble the Pizza

1. Spread an even layer of the beer cheese sauce over the dough.
2. Sprinkle shredded mozzarella and cheddar cheese over the sauce.
3. Evenly distribute the caramelized onions and sliced

bratwurst across the pizza.

Bake the Pizza

1. Transfer the pizza onto the preheated stone or baking sheet.
2. Bake for 12-15 minutes or until the crust is golden and the cheese is bubbly.

Add Finishing Touches

1. Remove from the oven and drizzle with grainy mustard.
2. Garnish with fresh chopped parsley.
3. Slice and serve warm.

Nutritional Information (Per Serving)

- **Calories**: 520
- **Protein**: 24g
- **Fat**: 28g
- **Carbohydrates**: 45g
- **Fiber**: 3g
- **Sodium**: 940mg

A few years ago, I found myself at an Oktoberfest celebration, surrounded by the aroma of freshly baked pretzels, sizzling bratwurst, and creamy beer cheese. The combination of those warm, hearty flavors felt like the perfect comfort food. When I returned home, I knew I had to capture that experience in a pizza.

This German-inspired pizza brings all the flavors of an Oktoberfest feast onto a crispy pretzel-style crust. The beer cheese sauce is creamy and tangy, while the bratwurst and caramelized onions add the perfect amount of richness. Brushing the crust with a baking soda wash gives it that classic soft pretzel texture, and the grainy mustard drizzle ties everything together. Every bite feels like a celebration—hearty, flavorful, and perfect with an ice-cold beer.

Notes

- For extra pretzel flavor, brush the crust with melted butter after baking.
- Swap bratwurst for smoked kielbasa or German Weisswurst for a variation.
- Best served with a cold German beer or apple cider.

Southern BBQ Mac & Cheese Pizza

Serving Size: 4 servings
Prep Time: 25 minutes
Cook Time: 12-15 minutes
Total Time: 40 minutes

Ingredients
For the Mac & Cheese Topping

- 1 cup elbow macaroni
- 1 tablespoon unsalted butter
- 1 tablespoon all-purpose flour
- 1/2 cup whole milk
- 1/2 cup shredded sharp cheddar cheese
- 1/4 cup shredded Monterey Jack cheese
- 1/2 teaspoon garlic powder
- 1/4 teaspoon smoked paprika
- Salt and pepper to taste

For the BBQ Pulled Pork

- 1/2 pound pulled pork (pre-cooked or store-bought)
- 1/4 cup barbecue sauce (hickory-smoked or sweet-style)

For the Pizza Base

- 1 pizza dough (store-bought or homemade)
- 1 tablespoon olive oil

For the Toppings

- 1/2 cup shredded cheddar cheese
- 1/2 cup crispy fried onions

- 1 tablespoon chopped scallions

For Garnish

- Extra BBQ sauce for drizzling

Instructions
Prepare the Mac & Cheese

1. Cook the elbow macaroni according to package instructions. Drain and set aside.
2. In a saucepan, melt butter over medium heat and whisk in flour to form a roux.
3. Slowly add milk, stirring constantly, until the mixture thickens.
4. Stir in cheddar and Monterey Jack cheese, garlic powder, and smoked paprika until melted and smooth.
5. Season with salt and pepper to taste, then mix in the cooked macaroni. Remove from heat and set aside.

Prepare the BBQ Pulled Pork

1. In a small bowl, toss the pulled pork with barbecue sauce until evenly coated.
2. Warm in a skillet over low heat for 2-3 minutes, then set aside.

Prepare the Pizza Base

1. Preheat the oven to 475°F (245°C) and place a pizza stone or baking sheet inside to heat.
2. Roll out the pizza dough on a floured surface to your desired thickness.
3. Transfer to a parchment-lined surface and brush with olive

oil.

Assemble the Pizza

1. Spread an even layer of mac & cheese over the pizza dough.
2. Sprinkle shredded cheddar cheese over the top.
3. Evenly distribute the BBQ pulled pork across the pizza.

Bake the Pizza

1. Transfer the pizza onto the preheated stone or baking sheet.
2. Bake for 12-15 minutes or until the crust is golden and the cheese is bubbly.

Add Finishing Touches

1. Remove from the oven and top with crispy fried onions.
2. Sprinkle chopped scallions over the pizza.
3. Drizzle with extra barbecue sauce before serving.

Nutritional Information (Per Serving)

- **Calories**: 580
- **Protein**: 28g
- **Fat**: 29g
- **Carbohydrates**: 52g
- **Fiber**: 3g
- **Sodium**: 960mg

Growing up in the South, barbecue and mac & cheese were staples at every family gathering. I remember standing by the grill, watching the smoke curl up as the pulled pork slow-cooked to perfection. Meanwhile, inside, a pot of bubbling mac & cheese would be coming together, thick and creamy with just the right amount of tang from sharp cheddar.

The idea to merge these two dishes into a pizza came from a backyard cookout where I found myself layering pulled pork onto my mac & cheese. That moment sparked an idea—why not bring these two Southern classics together on a crispy pizza crust? The result was pure comfort food heaven. The smoky barbecue sauce blends perfectly with the creamy mac & cheese, while the crispy fried onions add a satisfying crunch. Now, whenever I make this pizza, it brings back memories of family gatherings, warm summer nights, and the unbeatable combination of cheesy, smoky, and crispy goodness.

Notes

- Try a spicy BBQ sauce for an extra kick.
- Swap pulled pork for shredded chicken or brisket for a different twist.
- Serve with coleslaw on the side for the full Southern experience.

British Shepherd's Pie Pizza

Serving Size: 4 servings
Prep Time: 30 minutes
Cook Time: 12-15 minutes
Total Time: 45 minutes

Ingredients
For the Mashed Potato Topping

- 2 medium russet potatoes, peeled and diced
- 2 tablespoons unsalted butter
- 1/4 cup whole milk
- 1/2 teaspoon salt
- 1/4 teaspoon black pepper
- 1/4 teaspoon garlic powder

For the Savory Meat Topping

- 1/2 pound ground lamb or beef
- 1/2 cup frozen peas
- 1/2 cup diced carrots
- 1/2 small onion, finely chopped
- 1 clove garlic, minced
- 1 tablespoon Worcestershire sauce
- 1/2 cup beef broth
- 1 tablespoon tomato paste
- 1 teaspoon fresh rosemary, chopped
- 1 teaspoon fresh thyme, chopped
- Salt and pepper to taste

For the Pizza Base

- 1 pizza dough (store-bought or homemade)

- 1 tablespoon olive oil

For Garnish

- 1/4 cup shredded cheddar cheese
- 1 tablespoon chopped fresh parsley

Instructions
Prepare the Mashed Potatoes

1. Boil the diced potatoes in salted water for about 15 minutes, until fork-tender.
2. Drain and mash with butter, milk, salt, black pepper, and garlic powder until smooth.
3. Set aside to cool slightly.

Prepare the Meat Topping

1. Heat a skillet over medium heat and cook the ground lamb or beef until browned. Drain excess fat.
2. Add onion, carrots, and garlic, cooking for another 3 minutes.
3. Stir in Worcestershire sauce, beef broth, tomato paste, rosemary, thyme, salt, and pepper.
4. Simmer for 5 minutes until the mixture thickens slightly. Stir in frozen peas and remove from heat.

Prepare the Pizza Base

1. Preheat the oven to 475°F (245°C) and place a pizza stone or baking sheet inside to heat.
2. Roll out the pizza dough on a floured surface to your desired thickness.
3. Transfer to a parchment-lined surface and brush with olive

oil.

Assemble the Pizza

1. Spread an even layer of the mashed potatoes over the pizza dough as the base.
2. Evenly distribute the meat mixture over the potatoes.
3. Sprinkle shredded cheddar cheese over the top.

Bake the Pizza

1. Transfer the pizza onto the preheated stone or baking sheet.
2. Bake for 12-15 minutes or until the crust is golden and the cheese is melted.

Add Finishing Touches

1. Remove from the oven and sprinkle with chopped fresh parsley.
2. Let cool for 2 minutes, then slice and serve warm.

Nutritional Information (Per Serving)

- **Calories**: 520
- **Protein**: 27g
- **Fat**: 22g
- **Carbohydrates**: 50g
- **Fiber**: 4g
- **Sodium**: 780mg

On a chilly winter evening in London, I had my first taste of a truly comforting Shepherd's Pie—a dish so warm and rich, it felt like a hug in food form. The layers of creamy mashed potatoes, seasoned meat, and melted cheese made it an instant favorite. That night, I found myself wondering how I could enjoy those same comforting flavors in a different way.

A few weeks later, back in my own kitchen, I decided to experiment by using mashed potatoes as a pizza base instead of traditional sauce. I spread the fluffy potatoes onto my dough, topped it with a rich meat filling, and finished it off with a sprinkling of cheddar. The result was the best of both worlds—crispy on the outside, creamy in the center, and packed with deep, savory flavors. Every bite reminds me of that cozy London night, sitting in a dimly lit pub with a warm plate of Shepherd's Pie and good company.

Notes

- Substitute ground beef with mushrooms and lentils for a vegetarian version.
- Try adding a drizzle of brown gravy for an extra layer of richness.
- Best served with a pint of dark ale or a classic English tea.

Swedish Meatball Pizza

Serving Size: 4 servings
Prep Time: 30 minutes
Cook Time: 12-15 minutes
Total Time: 45 minutes

Ingredients
For the Swedish Meatballs

- 1/2 pound ground beef
- 1/4 pound ground pork
- 1/4 cup breadcrumbs
- 1/4 teaspoon allspice
- 1/4 teaspoon nutmeg
- 1/2 teaspoon salt
- 1/4 teaspoon black pepper
- 1/2 teaspoon garlic powder
- 1/2 teaspoon onion powder
- 1 tablespoon milk
- 1 egg yolk
- 1 tablespoon butter (for cooking)

For the Swedish Cream Sauce (Pizza Base)

- 1 tablespoon butter
- 1 tablespoon all-purpose flour
- 1/2 cup beef broth
- 1/4 cup heavy cream
- 1 teaspoon Dijon mustard
- 1/4 teaspoon Worcestershire sauce
- Salt and pepper to taste

For the Pizza Base

- 1 pizza dough (store-bought or homemade)
- 1 tablespoon olive oil

For the Toppings

- 1 cup shredded mozzarella cheese
- 1/4 cup shredded Gruyère or Swiss cheese
- 6-8 Swedish meatballs, halved
- 1/4 cup lingonberry sauce (for drizzling)

For Garnish

- 1 tablespoon chopped fresh dill
- Extra black pepper

Instructions

Prepare the Swedish Meatballs

1. In a bowl, mix ground beef, ground pork, breadcrumbs, allspice, nutmeg, salt, pepper, garlic powder, onion powder, milk, and egg yolk until well combined.
2. Roll into small meatballs (about 1-inch in diameter).
3. Heat a skillet over medium heat, melt butter, and cook meatballs for 8-10 minutes, turning occasionally, until browned and cooked through.
4. Remove from heat and set aside.

Prepare the Swedish Cream Sauce

1. In the same skillet, melt butter and whisk in flour to form a roux.
2. Slowly add beef broth, whisking constantly until smooth.
3. Stir in heavy cream, Dijon mustard, and Worcestershire

sauce.

4. Simmer for 3-5 minutes until thickened. Season with salt and pepper.
5. Remove from heat and let cool slightly.

Prepare the Pizza Base

1. Preheat the oven to 475°F (245°C) and place a pizza stone or baking sheet inside to heat.
2. Roll out the pizza dough on a floured surface to your desired thickness.
3. Transfer to a parchment-lined surface and brush with olive oil.

Assemble the Pizza

1. Spread an even layer of the Swedish cream sauce over the dough.
2. Sprinkle shredded mozzarella and Gruyère over the sauce.
3. Evenly distribute the halved Swedish meatballs across the pizza.

Bake the Pizza

1. Transfer the pizza onto the preheated stone or baking sheet.
2. Bake for 12-15 minutes or until the crust is golden and the cheese is bubbly.

Add Finishing Touches

1. Remove from the oven and drizzle lingonberry sauce over the top.
2. Sprinkle with fresh dill and extra black pepper.

3. Slice and serve warm.

Nutritional Information (Per Serving)

- **Calories**: 540
- **Protein**: 28g
- **Fat**: 30g
- **Carbohydrates**: 45g
- **Fiber**: 3g
- **Sodium**: 850mg

The first time I had Swedish meatballs was at a cozy little café in Stockholm, where the air smelled of butter, herbs, and freshly baked bread. I was struck by how the creamy, slightly tangy sauce paired beautifully with the juicy, spiced meatballs, and the tart lingonberry jam balanced everything out with a sweet contrast. It was comfort food in its purest form.

Back home, I wanted to bring those same flavors into a different kind of dish, and pizza seemed like the perfect way to do it. The cream sauce acts as a luxurious base, the Swedish meatballs add richness, and the melted cheese ties it all together. But what really makes this pizza special is the lingonberry drizzle, which adds just the right amount of sweetness to balance the savory elements. Every bite reminds me of that snowy day in Stockholm, where I first discovered how truly comforting Swedish cuisine can be.

Notes

- Substitute lingonberry sauce with cranberry sauce if lingonberries are unavailable.
- Swap Gruyère for Parmesan or aged cheddar for a sharper bite.
- Best paired with a cold beer or spiced mulled wine.

Korean Kimchi & Spam Pizza

Serving Size: 4 servings
  Prep Time: 25 minutes
  Cook Time: 12-15 minutes
  Total Time: 40 minutes

Ingredients
For the Gochujang Cream Sauce (Pizza Base)

- 2 tablespoons mayonnaise
- 1 tablespoon sour cream
- 1 tablespoon gochujang (Korean chili paste)
- 1 teaspoon soy sauce
- 1 teaspoon honey
- 1 teaspoon rice vinegar

For the Pizza Base

- 1 pizza dough (store-bought or homemade)
- 1 tablespoon sesame oil

For the Toppings

- 1/2 cup kimchi, chopped and drained
- 1/2 can Spam, cut into small cubes
- 1 cup shredded mozzarella cheese
- 1/4 cup shredded cheddar cheese
- 1/2 teaspoon sesame seeds
- 2 scallions, sliced

For Garnish

- 1 teaspoon toasted sesame seeds

- 1 sheet nori (dried seaweed), cut into thin strips

Instructions

Prepare the Gochujang Cream Sauce

1. In a small bowl, whisk together mayonnaise, sour cream, gochujang, soy sauce, honey, and rice vinegar until smooth.
2. Set aside to allow flavors to meld.

Prepare the Pizza Base

1. Preheat the oven to 475°F (245°C) and place a pizza stone or baking sheet inside to heat.
2. Roll out the pizza dough on a floured surface to your desired thickness.
3. Transfer to a parchment-lined surface and brush with sesame oil.

Assemble the Pizza

1. Spread an even layer of the gochujang cream sauce over the dough.
2. Sprinkle shredded mozzarella and cheddar cheese over the sauce.
3. Evenly distribute the chopped kimchi and cubed Spam across the pizza.
4. Sprinkle with sesame seeds.

Bake the Pizza

1. Transfer the pizza onto the preheated stone or baking sheet.
2. Bake for 12-15 minutes or until the crust is golden and the cheese is bubbly.

Add Finishing Touches

1. Remove from the oven and sprinkle sliced scallions and extra sesame seeds over the top.
2. Garnish with shredded nori for an extra umami boost.
3. Slice and serve warm.

Nutritional Information (Per Serving)

- **Calories**: 530
- **Protein**: 24g
- **Fat**: 30g
- **Carbohydrates**: 46g
- **Fiber**: 3g
- **Sodium**: 910mg

The combination of kimchi and Spam is a nostalgic comfort food for many, especially those who grew up with Korean or Hawaiian influences. The first time I had this combination was in a simple kimchi fried rice dish, and I was amazed at how the salty, crispy Spam complemented the tangy, slightly spicy kimchi. That meal was the inspiration for this pizza, blending those same bold flavors with gooey cheese and a crispy crust.

Bringing it all together is the gochujang cream sauce, which adds a creamy heat that ties everything together. The toasted sesame seeds and shredded nori on top elevate it with a final umami burst, making every bite feel layered and satisfying. Now, every time I make this pizza, it reminds me of comforting home-cooked meals that blend old-school ingredients with modern creativity.

Notes

- For extra crispiness, fry the Spam in a pan before adding it to the pizza.

- If you prefer extra heat, drizzle with sriracha or add red pepper flakes.
- Best served with an ice-cold Korean soju cocktail or a light beer.

Canadian Poutine Pizza

Serving Size: 4 servings
Prep Time: 30 minutes
Cook Time: 12-15 minutes
Total Time: 45 minutes

Ingredients
For the Brown Gravy (Pizza Base)

- 2 tablespoons unsalted butter
- 2 tablespoons all-purpose flour
- 1 cup beef broth
- 1 teaspoon Worcestershire sauce
- 1/2 teaspoon garlic powder
- 1/4 teaspoon black pepper
- Salt to taste

For the Pizza Base

- 1 pizza dough (store-bought or homemade)
- 1 tablespoon olive oil

For the Toppings

- 1 cup cheese curds
- 1/2 cup French fries, cooked and crispy
- 1/2 cup shredded mozzarella cheese
- 1/4 cup crispy bacon bits (optional)
- 1 teaspoon fresh thyme leaves

For Garnish

- Extra black pepper

- 1 tablespoon chopped fresh parsley

Instructions
Prepare the Brown Gravy

1. In a small saucepan over medium heat, melt the butter.
2. Whisk in the flour and cook for 1-2 minutes until golden brown.
3. Slowly add the beef broth while whisking to prevent lumps.
4. Stir in Worcestershire sauce, garlic powder, black pepper, and salt.
5. Simmer for 3-5 minutes until thickened, then remove from heat.

Prepare the Pizza Base

1. Preheat the oven to 475°F (245°C) and place a pizza stone or baking sheet inside to heat.
2. Roll out the pizza dough on a floured surface to your desired thickness.
3. Transfer to a parchment-lined surface and brush with olive oil.

Assemble the Pizza

1. Spread an even layer of brown gravy over the pizza dough as the base sauce.
2. Sprinkle shredded mozzarella cheese over the gravy.
3. Evenly distribute the crispy French fries across the pizza.
4. Scatter cheese curds on top.
5. Sprinkle bacon bits (if using) and fresh thyme leaves.

Bake the Pizza

1. Transfer the pizza onto the preheated stone or baking sheet.
2. Bake for 12-15 minutes or until the crust is golden and the cheese is melted.

Add Finishing Touches

1. Remove from the oven and let cool for 2 minutes.
2. Sprinkle with extra black pepper and fresh parsley.
3. Slice and serve warm.

Nutritional Information (Per Serving)

- **Calories**: 580
- **Protein**: 26g
- **Fat**: 30g
- **Carbohydrates**: 52g
- **Fiber**: 3g
- **Sodium**: 890mg

Poutine is one of Canada's most iconic comfort foods, and for good reason—there's nothing quite like the combination of crispy fries, melty cheese curds, and rich brown gravy. The first time I had poutine was at a small diner in Montreal, and it instantly became one of my favorite indulgent meals. It was simple, yet so satisfying, with each bite offering a balance of crunch, creaminess, and deep, savory flavor.

This pizza is my take on that classic dish, transforming it into something even more fun to eat. The brown gravy acts as a deliciously rich sauce, while the crispy fries add an unexpected crunch. Cheese curds melt into gooey pockets of flavor, making each slice taste like the best parts of poutine, but with the bonus of a golden, crispy crust. Whether you're a poutine purist or just love unique pizza flavors, this one is sure to become a new favorite.

Notes

- For an extra indulgent twist, drizzle with extra gravy just before serving.
- Swap out bacon for grilled mushrooms to keep it vegetarian.
- Best paired with a cold Canadian lager or a classic maple whiskey cocktail.

Argentine Choripán Pizza

Serving Size: 4 servings
Prep Time: 25 minutes
Cook Time: 12-15 minutes
Total Time: 40 minutes

Ingredients

For the Chimichurri Sauce (Pizza Base & Garnish)

- 1/2 cup fresh parsley, finely chopped
- 2 tablespoons fresh oregano, finely chopped
- 3 cloves garlic, minced
- 1/4 teaspoon red pepper flakes
- 1/2 teaspoon salt
- 1/4 teaspoon black pepper
- 1/4 cup olive oil
- 2 tablespoons red wine vinegar

For the Pizza Base

- 1 pizza dough (store-bought or homemade)
- 1 tablespoon olive oil

For the Toppings

- 1/2 pound Argentine-style chorizo, grilled and sliced
- 1/2 cup roasted red peppers, sliced
- 1 cup shredded mozzarella cheese
- 1/4 cup crumbled queso fresco or feta
- 1 teaspoon smoked paprika

For Garnish

- Extra chimichurri drizzle
- Fresh oregano leaves

Instructions
Prepare the Chimichurri Sauce

1. In a small bowl, combine parsley, oregano, garlic, red pepper flakes, salt, black pepper, olive oil, and red wine vinegar.
2. Stir well and let sit for at least 10 minutes to allow flavors to meld.

Prepare the Pizza Base

1. Preheat the oven to 475°F (245°C) and place a pizza stone or baking sheet inside to heat.
2. Roll out the pizza dough on a floured surface to your desired thickness.
3. Transfer to a parchment-lined surface and brush with olive oil.

Assemble the Pizza

1. Spread half of the chimichurri sauce over the pizza dough as the base sauce.
2. Sprinkle shredded mozzarella cheese evenly over the chimichurri.
3. Evenly distribute the grilled chorizo slices and roasted red peppers across the pizza.
4. Sprinkle crumbled queso fresco and smoked paprika over the top.

Bake the Pizza

1. Transfer the pizza onto the preheated stone or baking sheet.
2. Bake for 12-15 minutes or until the crust is golden and the cheese is bubbly.

Add Finishing Touches

1. Remove from the oven and drizzle with the remaining chimichurri sauce.
2. Garnish with fresh oregano leaves for extra brightness.
3. Slice and serve warm.

Nutritional Information (Per Serving)

- **Calories**: 540
- **Protein**: 29g
- **Fat**: 28g
- **Carbohydrates**: 45g
- **Fiber**: 3g
- **Sodium**: 870mg

Argentina is known for its love of grilled meats, and choripán is one of its most famous street foods. A classic choripán consists of grilled chorizo sausage served on a crusty roll and topped with vibrant chimichurri sauce. The first time I had choripán was at a bustling outdoor market in Buenos Aires, where the smoky aroma of sizzling chorizo filled the air. The balance of bold, spicy sausage and herbaceous chimichurri was unforgettable, and I knew I had to find a way to capture those flavors in a pizza.

This pizza does exactly that. The chimichurri acts as both the base sauce and the finishing drizzle, ensuring every bite is packed with fresh, garlicky flavor. The grilled chorizo provides a smoky richness, while the roasted red peppers add a hint of sweetness. The crumbled queso fresco rounds it out with a creamy, salty contrast. This pizza is bold, satisfying, and full of Argentine spirit, making it perfect for anyone who loves smoky, herby flavors.

Notes

- For a spicier version, use spicy Argentine chorizo or add extra red pepper flakes.
- Chimichurri can be made in advance and stored in the fridge for up to 3 days.
- Best paired with a glass of Malbec or an ice-cold Quilmes beer.

Japanese Okonomiyaki Pizza

Serving Size: 4 servings
Prep Time: 25 minutes
Cook Time: 12-15 minutes
Total Time: 40 minutes

Ingredients
For the Okonomiyaki Sauce (Pizza Base)

- 2 tablespoons ketchup
- 1 tablespoon Worcestershire sauce
- 1 tablespoon oyster sauce
- 1 teaspoon soy sauce
- 1 teaspoon honey

For the Pizza Base

- 1 pizza dough (store-bought or homemade)
- 1 tablespoon olive oil

For the Toppings

- 1/2 cup shredded green cabbage
- 4 slices cooked bacon, chopped
- 1/2 cup shredded mozzarella cheese
- 1/4 cup shredded cheddar cheese
- 1/2 teaspoon black sesame seeds

For Garnish

- 2 tablespoons Kewpie mayonnaise (Japanese mayo)
- 1/4 cup bonito flakes
- 1 sheet nori (dried seaweed), cut into thin strips

- 2 scallions, thinly sliced
- 1 teaspoon toasted sesame seeds

Instructions
Prepare the Okonomiyaki Sauce

1. In a small bowl, whisk together ketchup, Worcestershire sauce, oyster sauce, soy sauce, and honey.
2. Stir until smooth and set aside.

Prepare the Pizza Base

1. Preheat the oven to 475°F (245°C) and place a pizza stone or baking sheet inside to heat.
2. Roll out the pizza dough on a floured surface to your desired thickness.
3. Transfer to a parchment-lined surface and brush with olive oil.

Assemble the Pizza

1. Spread an even layer of okonomiyaki sauce over the pizza dough as the base sauce.
2. Sprinkle shredded mozzarella and cheddar cheese evenly over the sauce.
3. Evenly distribute the shredded cabbage and cooked bacon over the pizza.
4. Sprinkle with black sesame seeds for added crunch.

Bake the Pizza

1. Transfer the pizza onto the preheated stone or baking sheet.
2. Bake for 12-15 minutes or until the crust is golden and the

cheese is bubbly.

Add Finishing Touches

1. Remove from the oven and drizzle Kewpie mayonnaise in a zigzag pattern across the pizza.
2. Sprinkle bonito flakes on top—the heat will make them "dance."
3. Garnish with shredded nori, sliced scallions, and toasted sesame seeds.
4. Slice and serve warm.

Nutritional Information (Per Serving)

- **Calories**: 510
- **Protein**: 25g
- **Fat**: 28g
- **Carbohydrates**: 45g
- **Fiber**: 3g
- **Sodium**: 890mg

Okonomiyaki is one of Japan's most beloved comfort foods, a savory cabbage pancake loaded with toppings and bursting with umami. The first time I had it was at a tiny street stall in Osaka, where the chef cooked everything on a sizzling teppan grill. As soon as the pancake was ready, he drizzled it with sweet-savory okonomiyaki sauce and creamy Kewpie mayo, then topped it with bonito flakes that danced in the heat. It was love at first bite.

Bringing those flavors to pizza felt like a natural fusion. The crispy crust mimics the pancake, while the shredded cabbage adds freshness and crunch. The bacon provides a smoky richness, and the bonito flakes and nori bring a deep umami boost. The finishing drizzle of Kewpie mayo and sesame seeds completes the dish, making every bite taste like a blend of Japanese tradition and pizza indulgence. If you love bold flavors and unique textures, this pizza is a must-try!

Notes

- For an authentic okonomiyaki flavor, use dried shrimp or tempura bits instead of bacon.
- If you can't find bonito flakes, substitute with a drizzle of extra soy sauce for umami.
- Best paired with a cold Japanese beer or a matcha lemonade.

Sweet Creations

1. **Fruit Pizza with Sugar Cookie Crust**: A delightful sugar cookie crust topped with a sweet cream cheese frosting and a colorful array of fresh fruit.

2. **Chocolate Calzone**: A warm, gooey chocolate-filled calzone dusted with powdered sugar and served with a scoop of vanilla ice cream.

3. **Tiramisu Pizza**: A pizza-inspired dessert with layers of coffee-soaked ladyfingers, mascarpone cheese, and cocoa powder.

4. **Grilled Stone Fruit with Honey and Yogurt**: Halved and grilled stone fruits (peaches, plums, apricots) drizzled with honey and served with a dollop of Greek yogurt.

5. **Cannoli Stuffed Crepes**: Thin crepes filled with a rich and creamy cannoli filling, garnished with mini chocolate chips and powdered sugar.

6. **Strawberry Balsamic Bruschetta**: Slices of toasted baguette topped with fresh strawberries, a drizzle of balsamic reduction, and a dollop of whipped cream.

7. **Lemon Ricotta Pizza with Berries**: A lemon-infused ricotta cheese spread on a pizza crust and topped with mixed berries and a drizzle of honey.

8. **S'mores Pizza**: A pizza covered in marshmallows, chocolate chips, and crushed graham crackers, toasted to perfection.

9. **Apple Galette with Cinnamon Caramel Sauce**: Rustic and flaky pastry filled with thinly sliced apples and drizzled with a warm cinnamon caramel sauce.

10. **Affogato with Biscotti**: A classic Italian dessert featuring a scoop of vanilla gelato or ice cream "drowned" in a shot of hot espresso, served with biscotti for dipping.

Fruit Pizza with Sugar Cookie Crust

Serving Size: 10 servings
   Prep Time: 20 minutes
   Cook Time: 15 minutes
   Cooling Time: 30 minutes
   Total Time: 1 hour 5 minutes

Ingredients
For the Sugar Cookie Crust:

- 1 1/4 cups all-purpose flour
- 1/2 teaspoon baking powder
- 1/4 teaspoon salt
- 1/2 cup (1 stick) unsalted butter, softened
- 3/4 cup granulated sugar
- 1 large egg
- 1 teaspoon vanilla extract

For the Cream Cheese Frosting:

- 8 ounces cream cheese, softened
- 1/4 cup unsalted butter, softened
- 1 cup powdered sugar
- 1 teaspoon vanilla extract

For the Fruit Topping:

- 1/2 cup strawberries, sliced
- 1/2 cup kiwi, peeled and sliced
- 1/4 cup blueberries
- 1/4 cup raspberries
- 1/4 cup mandarin orange segments (optional)
- 1 tablespoon apricot jam or honey (optional, for glaze)

Instructions

1. **Prepare the Sugar Cookie Crust:**
   - Preheat your oven to 350°F (175°C) and lightly grease a 12-inch pizza pan or line it with parchment paper.
   - In a medium bowl, whisk together the flour, baking powder, and salt. Set aside.
   - In a large mixing bowl, cream the softened butter and granulated sugar until light and fluffy, about 2-3 minutes.
   - Beat in the egg and vanilla extract until well combined.
   - Gradually add the dry ingredients to the wet ingredients, mixing until a soft dough forms.
   - Press the dough evenly onto the prepared pizza pan to form the crust.
   - Bake for 12-15 minutes, or until the edges are lightly golden. Allow the crust to cool completely, about 30 minutes.

2. **Make the Cream Cheese Frosting:**
   - In a medium bowl, beat the cream cheese and butter together until smooth and creamy.
   - Gradually add the powdered sugar and beat until well combined. Mix in the vanilla extract.

3. **Assemble the Fruit Pizza:**
   - Once the crust is completely cool, spread the cream cheese frosting evenly over the surface, leaving a small border around the edge.
   - Arrange the fresh fruit on top of the frosting in a decorative pattern. Start with larger slices and fill in with smaller fruits for a visually stunning

presentation.

- ○ If desired, warm the apricot jam or honey slightly and brush it over the fruit for a shiny glaze.

4. **Serve:**
   - ○ Slice into wedges and serve immediately. Store leftovers in the refrigerator for up to 2 days.

Nutritional Information (Per Serving)

- Calories: 280
- Protein: 3g
- Fat: 15g
  - ○ Saturated Fat: 9g
- Carbohydrates: 34g
  - ○ Fiber: 1g
  - ○ Sugar: 21g
- Sodium: 120mg
- Cholesterol: 55mg

Fruit Pizza with Sugar Cookie Crust is a dessert that always brings a sense of celebration to the table. I first made this dish for a summer potluck, inspired by the abundance of fresh, colorful fruit at the local farmers' market. Its bright, cheerful appearance and balance of sweetness and creaminess made it an instant crowd-pleaser.

The best part of this recipe is how customizable it is. You can use any combination of seasonal fruits, making it perfect year-round. The sugar cookie crust provides a buttery, slightly crisp base that contrasts beautifully with the creamy frosting and juicy fruit. The optional glaze adds a professional touch that makes it shine, both literally and figuratively.

Every time I make this fruit pizza, it's met with smiles and compliments. It's a dessert that not only tastes amazing but also brings people together, making it a staple for birthdays, picnics, and family gatherings. It's as much fun to make as it is to eat, with its creative and colorful design offering a chance to unleash your inner artist.

Notes

- *Fruit Selection*: Use a mix of colorful fruits like strawberries, kiwis, blueberries, and mandarin oranges for a visually appealing presentation. Swap with seasonal fruits like pomegranate seeds in winter or peaches in summer.
- *Customization*: Add a layer of lemon curd or a drizzle of honey over the cream cheese base for an extra burst of flavor.
- *Perfect for Parties*: For easy serving, create mini fruit pizzas using pre-cut sugar cookies as individual bases.
- *Make-Ahead Tip*: Prepare and chill the cookie crust and cream cheese base in advance, adding the fruit just before serving to prevent sogginess.

Chocolate Calzone

Serving Size: 6 servings
Prep Time: 15 minutes
Cook Time: 12 minutes
Total Time: 27 minutes

Ingredients
For the Dough:

- 1 pound pizza dough (store-bought or homemade)
- All-purpose flour (for dusting)

For the Filling:

- 1/2 cup semisweet or milk chocolate chips
- 1/4 cup mini marshmallows (optional, for a gooey texture)
- 2 tablespoons hazelnut spread (optional, for added richness)

For the Topping:

- 1 tablespoon unsalted butter, melted
- 1 tablespoon powdered sugar (for dusting)

For Serving:

- 4-6 scoops vanilla ice cream
- Chocolate sauce or caramel sauce (optional, for drizzling)

Instructions

1. **Preheat the Oven:**
   - Preheat your oven to 475°F (245°C) and line a baking sheet with parchment paper or grease

lightly with butter.

2. **Prepare the Dough:**
    - Lightly flour a clean surface and roll out the pizza dough into a large circle, about 12 inches in diameter. Cut into two smaller circles if making individual calzones.

3. **Assemble the Calzone:**
    - Spread the chocolate chips and mini marshmallows (if using) over one half of the dough, leaving a 1-inch border around the edges. Add a dollop of hazelnut spread for extra richness if desired.
    - Fold the dough over the filling to form a half-moon shape. Press the edges together firmly to seal, then crimp with a fork to ensure the filling stays inside during baking.

4. **Bake the Calzone:**
    - Transfer the calzone(s) to the prepared baking sheet. Brush the top with melted butter for a golden finish.
    - Bake in the preheated oven for 10-12 minutes, or until the crust is golden brown and puffed.

5. **Finish and Serve:**
    - Remove the calzone from the oven and let it cool for 2-3 minutes. Dust generously with powdered sugar.
    - Serve warm with a scoop of vanilla ice cream on the side. For extra decadence, drizzle with chocolate or caramel sauce before serving.

Nutritional Information (Per Serving)

- Calories: 280

- Protein: 5g
- Fat: 11g
  - Saturated Fat: 6g
- Carbohydrates: 39g
  - Fiber: 2g
  - Sugar: 18g
- Sodium: 200mg
- Cholesterol: 15mg

Chocolate Calzone is a dessert that turns any meal into an event. I was first introduced to this indulgent treat at an Italian restaurant during a celebratory dinner, and I was captivated by its gooey center and warm, crispy crust. Recreating it at home quickly became a passion project, especially when I realized how simple and customizable it could be.

The first time I served this dessert was at a family movie night. Watching everyone's faces light up as they broke into the calzone to reveal the melted chocolate and marshmallows was pure joy. The pairing with vanilla ice cream creates a perfect contrast between the warm pastry and the cold, creamy scoop.

This recipe has since become a favorite for special occasions, from birthdays to casual get-togethers. Its versatility allows for endless creativity—you can add fruits like strawberries or bananas, or experiment with different chocolates. It's a dessert that's easy to make but feels luxurious, and it never fails to bring smiles and sweet memories to the table.

Notes

- *Filling Ideas*: Experiment with fillings like Nutella, peanut butter, or caramel for different flavor profiles. Add chopped hazelnuts or crushed pretzels for crunch.
- *Serving Suggestions*: Pair with vanilla ice cream or drizzle

with raspberry sauce for a gourmet touch.

- *Sweet Dough Option*: Add a touch of sugar and vanilla extract to your pizza dough to create a subtly sweet crust.
- *Presentation Tip*: Sprinkle with powdered sugar or cocoa powder just before serving for an elegant finish.

Tiramisu Pizza

Serving Size: 8 servings
Prep Time: 20 minutes
Cook Time: 12 minutes
Total Time: 32 minutes

Ingredients
For the Crust:

- 1 pound pizza dough (store-bought or homemade)
- 1 tablespoon butter, melted

For the Tiramisu Topping:

- 1/2 cup brewed espresso or strong coffee, cooled
- 2 tablespoons coffee liqueur (optional, for added flavor)
- 8 ounces mascarpone cheese, softened
- 1/2 cup heavy cream
- 1/3 cup powdered sugar
- 1 teaspoon vanilla extract
- 6-8 ladyfingers, broken into pieces
- 1/4 cup cocoa powder (for dusting)
- 1/4 cup grated dark chocolate or chocolate curls (optional, for garnish)

Instructions

1. **Prepare the Pizza Crust:**
   - Preheat your oven to 475°F (245°C) and line a pizza stone or baking sheet with parchment paper.
   - Roll out the pizza dough into a 12-inch circle and transfer it to the prepared baking surface.
   - Brush the crust with melted butter to give it a

soft, rich finish.

   ◦ Bake for 10-12 minutes, or until the crust is golden and cooked through. Allow to cool completely.

2. **Prepare the Mascarpone Mixture:**
   ◦ In a mixing bowl, whip the mascarpone cheese, heavy cream, powdered sugar, and vanilla extract until smooth and slightly fluffy. Set aside.

3. **Assemble the Tiramisu Layers:**
   ◦ In a shallow dish, combine the brewed espresso and coffee liqueur (if using). Quickly dip the ladyfinger pieces into the coffee mixture, ensuring they are soaked but not soggy.
   ◦ Spread a generous layer of the mascarpone mixture over the cooled pizza crust.
   ◦ Arrange the soaked ladyfinger pieces evenly on top of the mascarpone layer.
   ◦ Spread another thin layer of the mascarpone mixture over the ladyfingers to cover them completely.

4. **Finish with Cocoa Powder and Garnish:**
   ◦ Dust the top of the pizza generously with cocoa powder.
   ◦ Sprinkle grated dark chocolate or chocolate curls over the top for extra indulgence.

5. **Chill and Serve:**
   ◦ Refrigerate the assembled tiramisu pizza for at least 1 hour to allow the flavors to meld and the mascarpone layer to set.
   ◦ Slice and serve chilled for a unique and elegant dessert.

Nutritional Information (Per Serving)

- Calories: 280
- Protein: 4g
- Fat: 15g
    - Saturated Fat: 9g
- Carbohydrates: 30g
    - Fiber: 1g
    - Sugar: 14g
- Sodium: 150mg
- Cholesterol: 50mg

Tiramisu Pizza is a whimsical fusion of two beloved classics that brings a playful yet elegant twist to dessert. The inspiration came from my love of tiramisu paired with the idea of creating a dessert pizza that could shine at gatherings. The first time I made it, I wasn't sure if it would work—but it was a massive hit.

The balance of the soft, buttery crust with the creamy mascarpone, rich coffee-soaked ladyfingers, and a dusting of cocoa powder creates layers of flavor and texture that mimic the classic Italian dessert. It's indulgent yet light, making it perfect for ending a meal on a high note.

Every time I serve this tiramisu pizza, it's met with delight and curiosity, often sparking conversations about favorite desserts. It's a recipe that combines comfort with creativity, proving that the best dishes often come from blending the familiar with the unexpected.

Notes

- *Coffee Layer Tips*: Brush the pizza dough generously with the coffee and liqueur mixture, ensuring it soaks in for maximum flavor.
- *Mascarpone Variations*: For a lighter topping, fold whipped

cream into the mascarpone mixture before spreading it onto the crust.

- *Garnish Options*: Dust with cocoa powder and shaved dark chocolate for a classic tiramisu look. Add chocolate-covered espresso beans for a crunch.
- *Make It Ahead*: Assemble the pizza, except for the cocoa dusting, up to 1 hour in advance. Add the cocoa and serve chilled for a refreshing dessert.

Grilled Stone Fruit with Honey and Yogurt

Serving Size: 4 servings
Prep Time: 10 minutes
Cook Time: 6 minutes
Total Time: 16 minutes

Ingredients
For the Grilled Fruit:

- 2 large peaches, halved and pitted
- 2 plums, halved and pitted
- 4 apricots, halved and pitted
- 1 tablespoon olive oil or melted butter (for brushing)
- 1/4 teaspoon cinnamon (optional)

For the Topping:

- 4 tablespoons honey
- 1 cup Greek yogurt (full-fat or low-fat)
- 1/4 cup granola or chopped nuts (optional, for garnish)
- Fresh mint leaves (optional, for garnish)

Instructions

1. **Prepare the Fruit:**
   - Preheat your grill or grill pan to medium-high heat.
   - Brush the cut sides of the stone fruits lightly with olive oil or melted butter to prevent sticking. If desired, sprinkle a touch of cinnamon on the cut sides for extra flavor.

2. **Grill the Fruit:**
   - Place the fruit halves cut side down on the preheated grill. Grill for 3-4 minutes, or until the fruit develops visible grill marks and begins to soften slightly.
   - Flip the fruit and grill the skin side for an additional 2 minutes, or until warmed through. Remove from the grill and set aside.
3. **Assemble the Dish:**
   - Arrange the grilled fruit halves on a serving platter or individual plates.
   - Drizzle each piece with honey, allowing it to seep into the warm fruit.
   - Add a dollop of Greek yogurt to each serving. Sprinkle with granola or chopped nuts for crunch, if desired, and garnish with fresh mint leaves for a pop of color.
4. **Serve:**
   - Serve immediately while the fruit is warm, letting the creamy yogurt and sweet honey complement the smoky, caramelized fruit.

Nutritional Information (Per Serving)

- Calories: 150
- Protein: 6g
- Fat: 3g
   - Saturated Fat: 1g
- Carbohydrates: 28g
   - Fiber: 2g
   - Sugar: 22g
- Sodium: 20mg
- Cholesterol: 5mg

Grilled Stone Fruit with Honey and Yogurt is a dessert that celebrates the beauty of simple, fresh ingredients. The inspiration for this dish came during a summer barbecue when I wanted to create a dessert that felt light yet indulgent. The idea of grilling stone fruits was both practical and transformative—the natural sweetness of the fruit deepened, and the slight smokiness added complexity.

The first time I made this dish, the combination of warm, caramelized fruit with cool, creamy yogurt and a drizzle of honey won everyone over. It was a crowd-pleaser that felt elegant yet effortless, perfect for warm evenings under the stars.

What I love most about this recipe is its versatility. You can swap in different fruits, adjust the toppings to suit your preferences, or even serve it with ice cream for a more indulgent version. Each bite is a reminder that the best desserts often come from nature itself, enhanced by a touch of creativity and care.

Notes

- *Stone Fruit Options*: Peaches, plums, apricots, and nectarines grill beautifully. For extra sweetness, sprinkle them with a touch of brown sugar before grilling.
- *Yogurt Variations*: Swap Greek yogurt with mascarpone, crème fraîche, or coconut yogurt for added richness or a dairy-free option.
- *Flavor Enhancements*: Add a sprinkle of cinnamon or a few fresh mint leaves for a fresh, aromatic touch.
- *Presentation*: Serve on a platter with the fruit halves arranged in a circle and yogurt drizzled in the center for a stunning display.

Cannoli Stuffed Crepes

Serving Size: 8 servings
Prep Time: 20 minutes
Cook Time: 15 minutes
Total Time: 35 minutes

Ingredients
For the Crepes:

- 1 cup all-purpose flour
- 2 large eggs
- 1 1/2 cups whole milk
- 1 tablespoon granulated sugar
- 1 tablespoon unsalted butter, melted (plus extra for greasing the pan)
- 1/2 teaspoon vanilla extract
- Pinch of salt

For the Cannoli Filling:

- 1 cup ricotta cheese (drained if watery)
- 1/2 cup mascarpone cheese
- 1/2 cup powdered sugar (plus extra for garnish)
- 1/2 teaspoon vanilla extract
- 1/2 teaspoon orange zest (optional, for authentic flavor)
- 1/4 cup mini chocolate chips (plus extra for garnish)

Instructions

1. **Prepare the Crepe Batter:**
   - In a mixing bowl, whisk together the flour, sugar, and salt.
   - In a separate bowl, whisk the eggs, milk, melted

butter, and vanilla extract until well combined. Gradually add the wet ingredients to the dry ingredients, whisking until smooth and lump-free.

- Let the batter rest for 10 minutes to allow the flour to hydrate.

2. **Cook the Crepes:**
   - Heat a nonstick skillet or crepe pan over medium heat and lightly grease with butter.
   - Pour 1/4 cup of batter into the pan, swirling to spread it evenly into a thin circle. Cook for 1-2 minutes, or until the edges lift easily and the bottom is lightly golden. Flip and cook for another 30 seconds.
   - Transfer to a plate and repeat with the remaining batter, stacking the crepes with parchment paper in between to prevent sticking.

3. **Prepare the Cannoli Filling:**
   - In a medium bowl, whisk together the ricotta cheese, mascarpone cheese, powdered sugar, vanilla extract, and orange zest (if using) until smooth and creamy.
   - Fold in the mini chocolate chips. Refrigerate the filling until ready to use.

4. **Assemble the Cannoli Crepes:**
   - Lay a crepe flat on a clean surface. Spread about 2-3 tablespoons of the cannoli filling onto the center of the crepe, then fold the sides over the filling to create a neat roll or fold into quarters for a triangular shape. Repeat with the remaining crepes and filling.

5. **Garnish and Serve:**
   - Arrange the filled crepes on a serving platter. Dust

generously with powdered sugar and sprinkle with additional mini chocolate chips.

- ○ Serve immediately and enjoy the rich, creamy indulgence.

Nutritional Information (Per Serving)

- Calories: 230
- Protein: 6g
- Fat: 11g
    - ○ Saturated Fat: 7g
- Carbohydrates: 25g
    - ○ Fiber: 1g
    - ○ Sugar: 12g
- Sodium: 100mg
- Cholesterol: 60mg

Cannoli Stuffed Crepes are the perfect marriage of two beloved desserts, blending the delicate elegance of crepes with the rich, creamy filling of a classic Italian cannoli. The inspiration for this dish came during a brunch gathering where I wanted to create something unique yet comforting. Combining two favorites into one dish was a gamble that paid off beautifully.

The first time I served these, I was amazed at how quickly they disappeared from the platter. Guests loved the subtle sweetness of the filling, complemented by the occasional bite of chocolate chips and the refreshing hint of orange zest. The dusting of powdered sugar added just the right amount of flair, making them as stunning to look at as they were to eat.

What makes this recipe special is its versatility. You can adjust the filling's sweetness, experiment with toppings like crushed pistachios, or even drizzle with chocolate sauce for an extra touch.

Every time I make these cannoli stuffed crepes, they bring a sense of joy and indulgence, proving that the best desserts are those that bring smiles with every bite.

Notes

- *Ricotta Filling Tips*: Strain the ricotta cheese overnight to remove excess moisture, resulting in a smoother, creamier filling.
- *Flavor Variations*: Add orange zest or a splash of almond extract for a traditional Sicilian twist.
- *Garnish Suggestions*: Sprinkle with mini chocolate chips, crushed pistachios, or drizzle with melted chocolate for a sophisticated finish.
- *Make-Ahead Tip*: Crepes can be made ahead of time and stored between parchment paper in the fridge for up to 2 days. Assemble the cannoli filling and stuff just before serving.

Strawberry Balsamic Bruschetta

Serving Size: 12 servings
Prep Time: 15 minutes
Cook Time: 10 minutes
Total Time: 25 minutes

Ingredients
For the Balsamic Reduction:

- 1/2 cup balsamic vinegar
- 1 tablespoon honey or brown sugar (optional, for sweetness)

For the Strawberry Topping:

- 1 cup fresh strawberries, diced
- 1 teaspoon sugar (optional, to enhance sweetness)
- 1/2 teaspoon fresh lemon juice

For the Baguette:

- 1 French baguette, sliced into 1/2-inch rounds (about 12 slices)
- 2 tablespoons unsalted butter or olive oil, for brushing

For the Whipped Cream:

- 1/2 cup heavy cream
- 1 tablespoon powdered sugar
- 1/2 teaspoon vanilla extract

For Garnish:

- Fresh mint leaves (optional)

1. **Prepare the Balsamic Reduction:**
   - In a small saucepan, bring the balsamic vinegar to a gentle simmer over medium heat. Stir in honey or brown sugar if using.
   - Reduce the heat to low and let the mixture simmer for 8-10 minutes, stirring occasionally, until thickened and syrupy. Remove from heat and let cool.
2. **Prepare the Strawberry Topping:**
   - In a small bowl, combine the diced strawberries, sugar (if using), and lemon juice. Toss gently to coat and set aside.
3. **Toast the Baguette:**
   - Preheat your oven to 375°F (190°C). Arrange the baguette slices on a baking sheet and brush each slice with butter or olive oil.
   - Toast in the oven for 6-8 minutes, flipping halfway through, until golden and crisp. Let cool slightly.
4. **Whip the Cream:**
   - In a chilled mixing bowl, beat the heavy cream with powdered sugar and vanilla extract until soft peaks form. Keep refrigerated until ready to use.
5. **Assemble the Bruschetta:**
   - Spoon a generous amount of the strawberry topping onto each toasted baguette slice.
   - Drizzle with the cooled balsamic reduction. Add a dollop of whipped cream on top of each bruschetta.
6. **Garnish and Serve:**

- Garnish with fresh mint leaves for a pop of color and a hint of freshness. Arrange the bruschetta on a serving platter and serve immediately.

Nutritional Information (Per Serving)

- Calories: 110
- Protein: 2g
- Fat: 5g
  - Saturated Fat: 3g
- Carbohydrates: 13g
  - Fiber: 1g
  - Sugar: 4g
- Sodium: 50mg
- Cholesterol: 15mg

Strawberry Balsamic Bruschetta is a delightful twist on the classic savory appetizer, turning it into a sweet and tangy treat. The inspiration for this recipe came from a spring garden party where I wanted to showcase the season's freshest strawberries in a way that felt elegant and unexpected.

The first time I made this dish, it was met with enthusiastic praise. Guests were surprised by how the sweet strawberries paired perfectly with the tangy balsamic reduction and the richness of whipped cream. The crispy, buttery baguette added the perfect textural contrast, making each bite a harmonious blend of flavors.

What I love most about this recipe is its versatility. It works equally well as a dessert, a unique appetizer, or even a brunch dish. The fresh, vibrant presentation always draws compliments, and its simplicity means I can spend more time enjoying the company of friends and family. This recipe is a celebration of seasonal ingredients and the joy of sharing something both delicious and beautiful.

Notes

- *Balsamic Reduction*: Use a high-quality balsamic vinegar and reduce it over low heat until syrupy. For extra flavor, add a touch of honey or vanilla during the reduction process.
- *Bread Options*: Use a baguette or rustic sourdough bread for sturdy slices that can hold the topping without becoming soggy.
- *Customization*: Swap strawberries for other fruits like blackberries, figs, or peaches depending on the season.
- *Elegant Presentation*: Garnish with edible flowers, fresh mint, or a dollop of mascarpone for a stunning finish.

Lemon Ricotta Pizza with Berries

Serving Size: 8 servings
Prep Time: 15 minutes
Cook Time: 12 minutes
Total Time: 27 minutes

Ingredients

For the Pizza Base:

- 1 pizza dough (store-bought or homemade)
- 1 tablespoon olive oil

For the Lemon Ricotta Spread:

- 1 cup ricotta cheese
- 1 tablespoon honey
- 1 teaspoon lemon zest
- 1 teaspoon fresh lemon juice
- 1/2 teaspoon vanilla extract

For the Toppings:

- 1/2 cup fresh blueberries
- 1/2 cup fresh raspberries
- 1/2 cup sliced strawberries
- 2 tablespoons honey (for drizzling)
- Fresh mint leaves (optional, for garnish)
- Powdered sugar (optional, for dusting)

Instructions

1. **Prepare the Pizza Base:**
   - Preheat your oven to 475°F (245°C) and line a

baking sheet or pizza stone with parchment paper.

- ○ Roll out the pizza dough into a 12-inch circle or rectangle and transfer it to the prepared baking surface.
- ○ Brush the dough lightly with olive oil to create a golden crust.

2. **Bake the Crust:**
   - ○ Bake the pizza crust in the preheated oven for 8-10 minutes, or until golden and crisp. Remove from the oven and allow it to cool slightly.

3. **Make the Lemon Ricotta Spread:**
   - ○ In a medium mixing bowl, whisk together the ricotta cheese, honey, lemon zest, lemon juice, and vanilla extract until smooth and creamy.

4. **Assemble the Pizza:**
   - ○ Spread the lemon ricotta mixture evenly over the cooled pizza crust, leaving a small border around the edges.
   - ○ Scatter the fresh berries evenly over the ricotta layer.

5. **Finish with Honey and Garnishes:**
   - ○ Drizzle the pizza with honey for a touch of sweetness. Garnish with fresh mint leaves and a light dusting of powdered sugar, if desired.

6. **Serve:**
   - ○ Slice the pizza and serve immediately. It's best enjoyed slightly warm or at room temperature.

Nutritional Information (Per Serving)

- Calories: 180
- Protein: 5g
- Fat: 6g

- ○ Saturated Fat: 3g
- Carbohydrates: 24g
  - ○ Fiber: 2g
  - ○ Sugar: 8g
- Sodium: 150mg
- Cholesterol: 10mg

Lemon Ricotta Pizza with Berries is a dessert that brings together elegance and simplicity. The idea for this recipe came to me while hosting a summer brunch, where I wanted to offer a sweet yet refreshing option that showcased seasonal fruits. The combination of creamy ricotta, zesty lemon, and juicy berries felt like the perfect harmony of flavors.

The first time I served this pizza, the reaction was pure delight. Guests loved the unexpected combination of a crisp pizza crust with the creamy lemon ricotta and the burst of sweetness from the berries. The drizzle of honey and fresh mint added just the right finishing touches, making it as visually stunning as it was delicious.

What makes this recipe so special is its versatility. It works as a dessert, a brunch item, or even a light snack on a warm day. Every time I make this dish, I'm reminded of the joy that simple, fresh ingredients can bring, turning a humble pizza into a delightful celebration of flavor and creativity.

Notes

- *Berries Selection*: Use a mix of berries for contrast, such as raspberries for tartness and blackberries for sweetness.
- *Ricotta Tips*: Whip the ricotta with a touch of honey or vanilla extract for a creamier, dessert-like texture.
- *Flavor Boost*: Drizzle the pizza with lemon curd or a citrus glaze for a zesty, sweet topping.
- *Serving Suggestion*: Serve warm for a cozy dessert or chilled

for a refreshing summer treat.

S'mores Pizza

Serving Size: 8 servings
    Prep Time: 10 minutes
    Cook Time: 10-12 minutes
    Total Time: 22 minutes

Ingredients

For the Pizza Base:

- 1 pound pizza dough (store-bought or homemade)
- 1 tablespoon butter, melted

For the Toppings:

- 1/2 cup chocolate hazelnut spread or melted semisweet chocolate
- 1 cup mini marshmallows
- 1/2 cup semisweet or milk chocolate chips
- 1/2 cup crushed graham crackers
- 1 teaspoon powdered sugar (optional, for garnish)

Instructions

1. **Prepare the Pizza Dough:**
   - Preheat your oven to 475°F (245°C) and line a baking sheet or pizza stone with parchment paper.
   - Roll out the pizza dough into a 12-inch circle or rectangle and transfer it to the prepared baking surface.
   - Brush the dough with melted butter to enhance the flavor and create a golden crust.
2. **Bake the Crust:**
   - Bake the pizza crust in the preheated oven for 8

minutes, or until it is lightly golden and just firm.
Remove from the oven and let it cool slightly.

3. **Assemble the Toppings:**
    - Spread the chocolate hazelnut spread or melted chocolate evenly over the pre-baked crust, leaving a small border around the edges.
    - Sprinkle the mini marshmallows, chocolate chips, and crushed graham crackers evenly over the chocolate layer.

4. **Final Bake and Toast:**
    - Return the pizza to the oven and bake for an additional 3-4 minutes, or until the marshmallows are puffed and golden. Keep a close eye to prevent burning.
    - If desired, use a kitchen torch to lightly toast the marshmallows for an extra smoky flavor.

5. **Garnish and Serve:**
    - Allow the pizza to cool for a minute or two, then dust lightly with powdered sugar for a touch of sweetness.
    - Slice and serve immediately while the marshmallows are gooey and the chocolate is melted.

Nutritional Information (Per Serving)

- Calories: 260
- Protein: 4g
- Fat: 10g
    - Saturated Fat: 5g
- Carbohydrates: 38g
    - Fiber: 1g
    - Sugar: 18g

- Sodium: 150mg
- Cholesterol: 10mg

S'mores Pizza is a dessert that brings the nostalgia of campfire nights to your table in the most indulgent way. The idea came to me during a family gathering where we were reminiscing about our favorite summer traditions. I wanted to recreate the classic s'mores experience in a fun and shareable format, and pizza felt like the perfect vehicle.

The first time I made this, the kitchen was filled with the delightful aroma of toasted marshmallows and melted chocolate, and it instantly drew everyone in. Watching my family's faces light up as they took their first bite, gooey marshmallow strings stretching from their fingers, was unforgettable.

What I love most about this recipe is its simplicity and how it sparks joy in both kids and adults. It's a playful, crowd-pleasing dessert that can be customized with extra toppings like peanut butter drizzle or caramel sauce. Every time I serve this, it feels like a celebration, turning any meal into a sweet and memorable occasion.

Notes

- *Marshmallow Toasting Tip*: For evenly toasted marshmallows, use the broiler for the last 1-2 minutes of baking or use a culinary torch.
- *Chocolate Choices*: Dark chocolate provides a rich flavor, but milk chocolate or white chocolate can be used for a sweeter option.
- *Topping Additions*: Add peanut butter drizzle or chopped nuts for an extra layer of flavor.
- *Presentation*: Serve on a wooden board lined with parchment paper for a rustic, campfire-inspired look.

Apple Galette with Cinnamon Caramel Sauce

Serving Size: 8 servings
Prep Time: 20 minutes
Cook Time: 40 minutes
Total Time: 1 hour

Ingredients
For the Galette Pastry:

- 1 1/4 cups all-purpose flour
- 1/2 teaspoon salt
- 1 teaspoon sugar
- 1/2 cup unsalted butter, cold and cubed
- 3-4 tablespoons ice water

For the Apple Filling:

- 3 medium apples (Granny Smith or Honeycrisp), peeled, cored, and thinly sliced
- 2 tablespoons granulated sugar
- 1 tablespoon all-purpose flour
- 1 teaspoon ground cinnamon
- 1/4 teaspoon ground nutmeg
- 1 teaspoon lemon juice

For the Cinnamon Caramel Sauce:

- 1/2 cup granulated sugar
- 3 tablespoons unsalted butter, cubed
- 1/4 cup heavy cream
- 1/2 teaspoon ground cinnamon
- Pinch of salt

For Assembly:

- 1 egg, beaten (for egg wash)
- 1 tablespoon raw or turbinado sugar (for sprinkling)

Instructions

1. **Prepare the Pastry Dough:**
   - In a large bowl, whisk together the flour, salt, and sugar.
   - Add the cold, cubed butter and cut it into the flour using a pastry cutter or your fingers until the mixture resembles coarse crumbs.
   - Gradually add ice water, 1 tablespoon at a time, mixing gently until the dough comes together. Do not overwork.
   - Shape the dough into a disk, wrap in plastic wrap, and refrigerate for at least 30 minutes.
2. **Prepare the Apple Filling:**
   - In a medium bowl, toss the sliced apples with sugar, flour, cinnamon, nutmeg, and lemon juice. Set aside.
3. **Prepare the Cinnamon Caramel Sauce:**
   - In a small saucepan, melt the sugar over medium heat, stirring occasionally until it turns a deep amber color.
   - Add the butter and stir until melted. Slowly pour in the heavy cream while stirring, being cautious of splatters.
   - Stir in the cinnamon and a pinch of salt. Cook for 1-2 minutes, then remove from heat and let cool slightly.
4. **Assemble the Galette:**

- ○ Preheat your oven to 375°F (190°C) and line a baking sheet with parchment paper.
  - ○ On a lightly floured surface, roll out the chilled dough into a rough 12-inch circle. Transfer to the prepared baking sheet.
  - ○ Arrange the apple slices in the center of the dough, leaving a 2-inch border around the edges. Drizzle 2-3 tablespoons of the caramel sauce over the apples.
  - ○ Fold the edges of the dough over the filling, pleating as needed to form a rustic crust. Brush the crust with the beaten egg and sprinkle with raw sugar.

5. **Bake the Galette:**
   - ○ Bake in the preheated oven for 35-40 minutes, or until the crust is golden brown and the apples are tender. Allow to cool for 10 minutes.

6. **Serve:**
   - ○ Drizzle the remaining cinnamon caramel sauce over the baked galette. Slice and serve warm or at room temperature, optionally with a scoop of vanilla ice cream.

Nutritional Information (Per Serving)

- Calories: 320
- Protein: 3g
- Fat: 17g
  - ○ Saturated Fat: 10g
- Carbohydrates: 40g
  - ○ Fiber: 2g
  - ○ Sugar: 20g
- Sodium: 120mg

- Cholesterol: 55mg

Apple Galette with Cinnamon Caramel Sauce is a dessert that combines rustic charm with indulgent flavors. The inspiration for this recipe came from childhood autumn afternoons spent apple-picking with family, followed by the aroma of baking pies filling the kitchen. The simplicity of a galette, with its free-form shape and buttery crust, feels both approachable and elegant.

The first time I made this galette was for a holiday dinner. Its golden, flaky crust and perfectly spiced apple filling quickly became the centerpiece of the dessert table. The warm caramel sauce added a luxurious touch, complementing the tartness of the apples and the richness of the pastry.

What I love most about this recipe is how it celebrates the beauty of imperfections. The rustic folds of the crust and the caramel drizzles make each galette uniquely beautiful. It's a dessert that brings warmth, comfort, and a sense of togetherness, making every bite a sweet reminder of cherished moments.

Notes

- *Apple Selection*: Use a combination of tart and sweet apples, such as Granny Smith and Honeycrisp, for a balanced flavor.
- *Rustic Appeal*: Don't worry about making the crust perfect—its uneven folds add to the galette's rustic charm.
- *Caramel Sauce Tip*: Use store-bought caramel for convenience or make your own with butter, brown sugar, and cream. Add a pinch of sea salt for a salted caramel twist.
- *Serving Idea*: Serve warm with a scoop of vanilla ice cream or a dollop of whipped cream for added indulgence.

Affogato with Biscotti

Serving Size: 4 servings
Prep Time: 5 minutes
Cook Time: 5 minutes
Total Time: 10 minutes

Ingredients
For the Affogato:

- 4 scoops vanilla gelato or ice cream
- 4 shots hot espresso (about 1/4 cup each) or 1 cup strong brewed coffee

For the Biscotti:

- 8 biscotti (store-bought or homemade)

Optional Garnishes:

- Whipped cream
- Shaved dark chocolate or cocoa powder
- Chopped toasted almonds

Instructions

1. **Prepare the Espresso:**
   - Brew fresh espresso using an espresso machine or stovetop Moka pot. If you don't have an espresso maker, brew strong coffee as a substitute. Keep it hot for serving.
2. **Assemble the Affogato:**
   - Place one scoop of vanilla gelato or ice cream into each serving glass or dessert bowl. Use chilled

glasses for a more refined presentation.

3. **Add the Espresso:**
   - Pour a shot of hot espresso (or 1/4 cup strong coffee) directly over the gelato in each glass. The heat of the espresso will partially melt the gelato, creating a creamy, rich mixture.

4. **Serve with Biscotti:**
   - Arrange two biscotti on a small plate alongside each glass for dipping. For added flavor, consider offering almond, chocolate, or pistachio biscotti.

5. **Garnish and Serve:**
   - For a fancier presentation, top the affogato with whipped cream, shaved chocolate, or a sprinkle of chopped toasted almonds. Serve immediately and enjoy the delightful contrast of hot and cold flavors.

Nutritional Information (Per Serving)

- Calories: 280
- Protein: 5g
- Fat: 12g
  - Saturated Fat: 7g
- Carbohydrates: 37g
  - Fiber: 1g
  - Sugar: 26g
- Sodium: 60mg
- Cholesterol: 50mg

Affogato with Biscotti is a dessert that epitomizes simplicity and elegance. I was introduced to this classic Italian treat during a visit to Rome, where I enjoyed it at a quaint café overlooking a bustling piazza. The rich, velvety gelato melting into the bold espresso felt like a perfect union of textures and flavors.

The first time I recreated this dessert at home, it was for a dinner party. Its quick preparation allowed me to focus on enjoying time with my guests rather than being tied to the kitchen. Watching everyone savor the hot and cold contrast, dipping their biscotti into the creamy mixture, reminded me of the joy that comes from sharing good food and company.

What makes this dessert so special is its versatility. You can customize it with flavored gelatos, different types of biscotti, or even a splash of liqueur like amaretto or Frangelico for an adult twist. It's a go-to recipe for when you want to impress without stress, bringing a little Italian charm to your table every time.

Notes

- *Espresso Variations*: Use flavored espresso, such as hazelnut or vanilla, for a unique twist.
- *Ice Cream Choices*: Substitute the classic vanilla gelato with salted caramel or chocolate for a more decadent treat.
- *Biscotti Pairing*: Match your biscotti flavor to the ice cream or espresso—for instance, almond biscotti complements vanilla, while chocolate biscotti enhances mocha flavors.
- *Make It Boozy*: Add a splash of coffee liqueur or amaretto to the espresso for an adult version of this Italian classic.

The Ultimate Pairing Guide: Elevate Your Pizza Experience

A well-made pizza is an experience in itself, but when paired with the right drink, it transforms into something truly unforgettable. The perfect pairing enhances the flavors, textures, and overall enjoyment of each bite, whether it's a bold red wine complementing a meaty pizza, a crisp beer cutting through rich cheese, or a refreshing lemonade balancing spicy toppings.

This guide will help you explore the best wine, beer, cocktails, and non-alcoholic beverages to pair with your pizzas—so you can create a complete dining experience every time.

Wine & Pizza Pairings

◇ **Red Wines** – Best for rich, meaty, and tomato-based pizzas.

◇ **White Wines** – Ideal for lighter, creamy, and veggie-forward pizzas.

◇ **Sparkling Wines** – Perfect for balancing salty, tangy, or spicy toppings.

Pizza Type	Wine Pairing	Why It Works
Classic Margherita	Chianti, Sangiovese	The tomato sauce's acidity is balanced by Chianti's bright red fruit flavors.
Pepperoni & Meat Lovers	Zinfandel, Syrah	These bold wines stand up to the richness of cured meats.
BBQ Chicken	Malbec, Shiraz	The smoky sweetness of BBQ sauce complements the dark fruit and spice notes of these wines.
White Pizzas (Garlic Cream, Ricotta, Pesto)	Chardonnay, Viognier	Buttery, creamy whites complement rich sauces without overpowering.
Spicy Pizzas (Jerk Shrimp, Kimchi & Spam, Harissa-based)	Riesling, Gewürztraminer	The slight sweetness and acidity balance the spice beautifully.
Mushroom & Truffle Pizzas	Pinot Noir, Nebbiolo	Earthy wines mirror the umami depth of mushrooms.
Sweet Pizzas (Chocolate, Fruit-Based)	Port, Moscato, Dessert Wines	A natural sweetness pairing that enhances the dessert flavors.

◇ **Pro Tip:** If in doubt, a dry, crisp Rosé pairs well with nearly every pizza.

Beer & Pizza Pairings

◇ **Lighter Beers (Pilsner, Lager, Kölsch)** – Refreshing and crisp, great for cheese and veggie pizzas.

◇ **Hoppy Beers (IPA, Pale Ale)** – Bold, citrusy, and slightly bitter, cutting through rich, fatty flavors.

◇ **Dark Beers (Stout, Porter, Brown Ale)** – Deep and roasty, great with BBQ and meaty pizzas.

Pizza Type	Beer Pairing	Why It Works
Neapolitan Margherita	Pilsner, Helles Lager	Light and crisp, allowing the fresh tomatoes and basil to shine.
BBQ Mac & Cheese Pizza	Amber Ale, Smoked Porter	Maltiness complements BBQ sauce, while smokiness enhances the cheese.
Poutine Pizza	Brown Ale, Dunkel	Malty depth balances the richness of fries and gravy.
Pepperoni & Sausage	IPA, West Coast Pale Ale	Hops cut through the grease and enhance spicy meats.
Buffalo Chicken Pizza	Wheat Beer, Hazy IPA	Fruity notes balance the heat of buffalo sauce.
Mushroom & Truffle Pizza	Belgian Dubbel, Saison	Earthy and slightly funky flavors pair beautifully with truffle.
Hawaiian Poke Pizza	Sour Ale, Gose	Tartness complements the fresh, salty seafood flavors.

◇ **Pro Tip:** If unsure, a crisp Pilsner or Pale Ale pairs with nearly every pizza.

Cocktail & Pizza Pairings

Cocktails bring a fun, playful element to pizza pairings, with the ability to complement or contrast flavors using herbs, citrus, and spirits.

Pizza Type	Cocktail Pairing	Why It Works
Spicy Jerk Shrimp Pizza	Spicy Margarita	The heat of jerk seasoning is enhanced by the spice and citrus of a margarita.
Truffle Mushroom Pizza	Old Fashioned	The richness of truffle and cheese pairs well with bourbon's smoky depth.
Carbonara Pizza	Aperol Spritz	The bright, citrusy bitterness cuts through the creamy sauce.
BBQ Chicken Pizza	Whiskey Sour	The smoky BBQ flavors pair well with whiskey's vanilla and spice notes.
Pineapple & Mango Pizzas	Piña Colada, Daiquiri	Tropical flavors complement the fruitiness of the pizza.
Kimchi & Spam Pizza	Korean Soju & Soda	A light, slightly sweet soju cocktail balances the spice and saltiness.
Chocolate Dessert Pizza	Espresso Martini	Rich coffee flavors enhance the chocolate elements.

◇ **Pro Tip:** If serving multiple pizzas, a simple Gin & Tonic or Classic Mojito pairs well with most styles.

Non-Alcoholic Pairings

For those who prefer non-alcoholic beverages, there are plenty of options that enhance the flavors of your pizza while providing a refreshing balance.

Tea Pairings

◇ **Peppermint Tea** – Perfect for rich and cheesy pizzas, helping cleanse the palate.

◇ **Chai Tea** – A great match for BBQ-based pizzas with its warm, spiced flavors.

◇ **Iced Green Tea** – Bright and earthy, pairing well with fresh veggie and seafood pizzas.

Lemonades & Sodas

◇ **Classic Lemonade** – The acidity cuts through greasy or spicy pizzas.

◇ **Hibiscus Lemonade** – Pairs beautifully with tropical or Caribbean-inspired pizzas.

◇ **Ginger Beer** – Complements bold, spicy pizzas like Buffalo Chicken or Jerk Shrimp.

◇ **Cola** – A traditional favorite, balancing salty, fatty flavors.

Flavored Waters & Juices

◇ **Cucumber-Lime Sparkling Water** – Refreshing and great for light pizzas like Margherita.

◇ **Apple Cider** – A cozy match for cheesy and autumn-inspired pizzas.

◇ **Orange & Cranberry Juice Mix** – A citrusy contrast to bold, meaty pizzas.

◇ **Pro Tip:** If hosting, offer a non-alcoholic sangria or mocktail bar to complement different pizza flavors.

How to Create a Well-Balanced Pizza & Drink Menu

If you're hosting a pizza night or pairing multiple pizzas, here's how to balance your drink selection:

✔ **For a Classic Italian Night** → Serve a Margherita Pizza with Chianti or a crisp Peroni beer.

✔ **For a Spicy & Bold Theme** → Pair Buffalo Chicken Pizza with a wheat beer or a spicy margarita.

✔ **For a Cozy Comfort Meal** → Serve BBQ Mac & Cheese Pizza with a brown ale or whiskey sour.

✔ **For a Fusion Feast** → Pair Korean BBQ Pizza with soju cocktails or a crisp lager.

✔ **For a Sweet Ending** → Serve Chocolate Pizza with espresso martinis or vanilla bean tea.

Pairing pizza with the right drink is all about balance and fun. There are no strict rules—just recommendations to enhance your meal. Whether you're sipping on a bold red wine, a crisp lager, or a refreshing iced tea, the key is to choose what you love and enjoy the experience.

So mix, match, and explore new flavors. Your perfect pizza pairing awaits! ◇◇

Cooking Tips & Troubleshooting: Mastering the Art of Pizza-Making

Making pizza at home is an exciting and rewarding experience, but even the best home cooks encounter challenges. Whether you're aiming for a perfectly crispy crust, avoiding a soggy center, or figuring out the best way to store leftovers, this guide will help troubleshoot common pizza-making issues and provide pro tips to elevate your pizzas every time.

Achieving the Perfect Crispy Crust

A crispy, golden crust is the hallmark of a great pizza, but achieving that crunch requires the right technique and tools.

✔ **Preheat Your Oven Properly** – A high oven temperature (450–500°F / 230–260°C) is essential. Always preheat your oven for at least 30 minutes before baking. If using a pizza stone or baking steel, heat it for at least 45 minutes for the best results.

✔ **Use a Pizza Stone or Baking Steel** – A hot surface is key to a crisp crust. Baking on a preheated pizza stone or steel transfers heat directly to the dough, mimicking the effect of a professional pizza oven.

✔ **Par-Bake for Extra Crispiness** – If your pizzas tend to be too soft in the center, pre-bake the dough alone for 5 minutes before adding sauce and toppings. This helps create a stronger base.

✔ **Roll or Stretch Your Dough Evenly** – Thick, uneven dough can bake inconsistently. Aim for a uniform thickness so the crust bakes evenly from edge to center.

✔ **Dust with Semolina or Cornmeal** – Before baking, lightly dust your pizza peel or baking sheet with semolina or cornmeal to prevent sticking and add extra crispiness to the bottom.

✔ **Don't Overload with Toppings** – Too many toppings trap steam and prevent the crust from crisping up. Stick to a moderate amount of sauce, cheese, and toppings for the best texture.

◇ **Pro Tip:** If you love an extra crispy crust, try brushing the edges with olive oil before baking or placing the pizza under the broiler for the last 1-2 minutes to get a perfectly golden top.

Fixing Soggy or Undercooked Dough

There's nothing worse than a pizza that's doughy or wet in the middle. Here's how to fix and prevent soggy pizza.

✔ **Don't Overdo the Sauce** – Too much sauce leads to excess moisture. A thin, even layer is best—start with ½ cup of sauce per 12-inch pizza and adjust as needed.

✔ **Use Low-Moisture Cheese** – Fresh mozzarella is delicious but contains a lot of water. If using it, drain and pat dry before adding to the pizza. Low-moisture mozzarella is ideal for even melting and minimal moisture release.

✔ **Pre-Cook Watery Vegetables** – Ingredients like mushrooms, zucchini, and spinach release water as they cook. Sauté or roast them beforehand to remove excess moisture before adding them to your pizza.

✔ **Bake on the Right Surface** – If baking on a regular baking sheet, avoid parchment paper, as it can trap moisture. Instead, bake directly on the sheet or preheat the baking sheet for a crisper bottom.

✔ **Increase Baking Time for Thick-Crust Pizzas** – If using a thicker dough, reduce the oven temperature slightly to 425°F (220°C) and bake for a longer time to ensure the inside is fully cooked.

✔ **Check for Doneness** – The pizza is fully cooked when the bottom is golden brown and firm. If the toppings are done but the dough isn't, place the pizza on the lowest oven rack for 2-3 extra minutes to crisp the bottom.

◈ **Pro Tip:** If your pizza is still undercooked after baking, transfer it to a hot skillet for 2 minutes to crisp up the bottom without overcooking the toppings.

Best Ways to Store & Reheat Leftover Pizza

Proper storage and reheating ensure your pizza tastes just as good the next day.

How to Store Leftover Pizza

✔ **Refrigerate Properly** – Store pizza slices in an airtight container or wrap them in aluminum foil or parchment paper. This prevents them from absorbing fridge odors and drying out. Consume within 3–4 days for the best quality.

✔ **Freeze for Longer Storage** – Wrap individual slices in plastic wrap and foil, then store in a freezer-safe bag. Frozen pizza stays fresh for up to 2 months.

How to Reheat Pizza for Best Texture

◈ **Oven Method (Best for Crispiness)**

- Preheat oven to 375°F (190°C).
- Place pizza directly on a baking sheet or pizza stone.
- Bake for 7-10 minutes until the cheese is bubbly and the crust is crisp.

◈ **Skillet Method (Quick & Crispy)**

- Heat a non-stick or cast-iron skillet over medium heat.
- Place pizza slice in the pan and cover with a lid.
- Cook for 3-5 minutes until the bottom is crisp and the cheese is melty.

◈ **Air Fryer Method (Fast & Crunchy)**

- Set the air fryer to 350°F (175°C).
- Place slices in a single layer and heat for 3-5 minutes.

- Great for reviving crispy crusts!

◇ **Avoid the Microwave!** – It will make the crust soggy and chewy. If you must use it, place a small glass of water in the microwave with your slice to help reduce moisture absorption.

◇ **Pro Tip:** If reheating frozen pizza, let it thaw in the fridge overnight before using the oven or skillet methods.

Bonus Pro Tips for Next-Level Pizza

✔ **Rest Your Dough** – Always let dough rest for at least 30 minutes after refrigeration before shaping—it will be easier to stretch and won't shrink back.

✔ **Use a Cold Ferment for More Flavor** – Let dough rise in the fridge for 24-72 hours for deeper flavor and better texture.

✔ **Grate Your Own Cheese** – Pre-shredded cheese contains anti-caking agents that prevent proper melting. Freshly grated cheese melts better and has a richer flavor.

✔ **Bake with High Heat for a Charred Crust** – If possible, bake your pizza at 500°F (260°C) or higher for an authentic pizzeria-style crust.

✔ **Let Pizza Rest Before Slicing** – Give your pizza 2-3 minutes to cool before slicing—this helps keep toppings in place and prevents cheese from sliding off.

Pizza-making is an art and a science, and like any skill, it improves with practice. Every mistake is a learning opportunity, and with these troubleshooting tips, you'll be able to create crispy, perfectly baked pizzas every time.

The key is to experiment, have fun, and make each pizza your own. Whether you're trying out new dough styles, playing with different sauces, or crafting unique topping combinations, this book is your guide to becoming a pizza master! ◇◇◇

Index

This index will help you quickly find recipes by ingredient, type, and category, making it easy to navigate *Pizza Artistry: The Canvas of Flavor.* Whether you're looking for a specific pizza, a key ingredient, or a type of dough or sauce, this guide will direct you to the right recipe.

◈ **Recipe Index (Alphabetical Listing)**

A

- American Cheeseburger Pizza – *World Comfort Pizzas*
- Argentine Choripán Pizza – *World Comfort Pizzas*
- Artisan Bites & Starters (category introduction)

B

- British Shepherd's Pie Pizza – *World Comfort Pizzas*
- BBQ Pulled Pork & Pineapple Pizza – *Signature Pizzas*
- Beer Cheese Sauce – *Dough & Sauce Guide*
- Buffalo Chicken Pizza – *Signature Pizzas*

C

- Canadian Poutine Pizza – *World Comfort Pizzas*
- Caprese Salad with Balsamic Glaze – *Inspired Accompaniments*
- Carbonara Pizza (Italian) – *World Comfort Pizzas*
- Chimichurri Sauce – *Dough & Sauce Guide*
- Classic Tomato Sauce – *Dough & Sauce Guide*
- Chocolate Calzone – *Sweet Creations*

D

◈ **Ingredient-Based Index**

◈ **Bacon** – *See: Carbonara Pizza, Okonomiyaki Pizza, Buffalo Chicken Pizza*

◈ **BBQ Sauce** – *See: BBQ Pulled Pork & Pineapple Pizza, BBQ Mac & Cheese Pizza*

◈ **Beer Cheese** – *See: German Pretzel & Beer Cheese Pizza*

◈ **Bulgogi Beef** – *See: Korean BBQ Beef Pizza*

◈ **Caramelized Onions** – *See: German Pretzel Pizza, Poutine Pizza, Shepherd's Pie Pizza*

◇ **Cheese Curds** – *See: Poutine Pizza*

◇ **Chimichurri Sauce** – *See: Argentine Choripán Pizza*

◇ **Chocolate** – *See: Chocolate Calzone, Tiramisu Pizza, Nutella Dessert Pizza*

◇ **Chorizo** – *See: Argentine Choripán Pizza, Mexican Street Corn Pizza*

◇ **Crispy Fried Onions** – *See: BBQ Mac & Cheese Pizza*

◇ **Eggs** – *See: Carbonara Pizza, Okonomiyaki Pizza*

◇ **French Fries** – *See: Poutine Pizza*

◇ **Goat Cheese** – *See: Greek Spanakopita Pizza, Mediterranean Mezze Pizza*

◇ **Gochujang** – *See: Korean Kimchi & Spam Pizza, Korean BBQ Beef Pizza*

◇ **Gravy** – *See: Poutine Pizza, Shepherd's Pie Pizza*

◇ **Ground Beef** – *See: Cheeseburger Pizza, Shepherd's Pie Pizza, Swedish Meatball Pizza*

◇ **Kimchi** – *See: Korean Kimchi & Spam Pizza*

◇ **Lingonberry Sauce** – *See: Swedish Meatball Pizza*

◇ **Mac & Cheese** – *See: BBQ Mac & Cheese Pizza*

◇ **Mozzarella Cheese** – *See: All Pizza Recipes*

◇ **Mushrooms** – *See: French Ratatouille Pizza, Truffle Fries, Mushroom Ceviche*

◇ **Pancetta** – *See: Italian Carbonara Pizza*

◇ **Parmesan Cheese** – *See: Carbonara Pizza, Spinach & Artichoke Dip, Truffle Fries*

◇ **Peanut Sauce** – *See: Thai Peanut Chicken Pizza*

◇ **Pepperoni** – *See: Classic Pepperoni Pizza*

◇ **Pickles** – *See: Cheeseburger Pizza*

◇ **Pineapple** – *See: BBQ Pulled Pork & Pineapple Pizza, Hawaiian Poke Pizza*

◇ **Pomegranate Seeds** – *See: Moroccan Vegetable Tagine Pizza*

◇ **Prosciutto** – *See: Italian-Inspired Pizzas*

◇ **Red Peppers** – *See: Argentine Choripán Pizza, Greek Spanakopita Pizza, Mexican Street Corn Pizza*

◇ **Ricotta Cheese** – *See: Greek Spanakopita Pizza, White Garlic Pizzas*

◇ **Spam** – *See: Korean Kimchi & Spam Pizza*

◇ **Sweet Potatoes** – *See: Moroccan Vegetable Tagine Pizza*

◇ **Truffle Oil** – *See: Truffle Fries, Mushroom & Truffle Pizza*

About the Author

Food has always been more than just sustenance for me—it has been a way to connect, create, and explore the world through flavor. My journey into pizza-making didn't start in a culinary school or a professional kitchen. It started in my own home, where the scent of fresh dough rising in a warm oven and the excitement of crafting something entirely my own became a ritual of joy and creativity.

Growing up, pizza night was always something special. Whether it was a classic cheese pizza shared with family or a bold experiment with unexpected toppings, it became clear to me that pizza was more than just a meal—it was a blank canvas for endless possibilities. My passion for food led me to explore how different cultures interpreted this dish, and soon, I found myself creating pizzas that told stories, traveled continents, and blended flavors from around the world.

My love for fusion cuisine and artisan pizza-making is what inspired me to write *Pizza Artistry: The Canvas of Flavor*. I wanted to create a book that would empower home cooks—whether beginners or seasoned chefs—to think beyond the traditional, experiment with flavors, and craft pizzas that reflect their own creativity. From globally inspired toppings to decadent dessert pizzas, this book is a celebration of both tradition and innovation, proving that pizza can be whatever you want it to be.

Beyond the kitchen, I find inspiration in traveling, exploring markets filled with unfamiliar ingredients, and connecting with people through shared meals. Whether it's discovering the smoky depth of a perfectly grilled Argentine choripán or the umami explosion of a Japanese okonomiyaki, I believe that food has a way of bringing cultures together in ways that words cannot. That's what I hope to share with you in this book—the idea that food, and especially pizza, is a universal language of joy, creativity, and comfort.

I hope that *Pizza Artistry* not only teaches you how to perfect your dough, balance flavors, and master the craft of homemade pizza-making but also encourages you to be bold, play with ingredients, and make every pizza your own.

So go ahead—roll out your dough, fire up your oven, and create something unforgettable. After all, the best pizzas are the ones that tell a story.

Happy cooking, and may every slice be a masterpiece. ◈◈

Final Thank You & Encouragement

Thank you.

Thank you for joining me on this incredible journey through pizza, flavor, and creativity. Writing *Pizza Artistry: The Canvas of Flavor* has been a labor of love, inspired by the belief that pizza is more than just food—it's a form of self-expression, a way to connect with others, and a never-ending adventure in flavor.

I hope this book has inspired you to roll out your dough with confidence, experiment with sauces and toppings, and explore the rich traditions and bold innovations of pizza from around the world. Whether you've followed the recipes exactly or used them as a foundation for your own creative twists, I want you to know that there is no wrong way to make pizza. The best pizzas are the ones that reflect your taste, your experiences, and your unique approach to cooking.

I encourage you to keep experimenting, keep playing with flavors, and keep pushing the boundaries of what pizza can be. Try unexpected ingredient pairings, test new techniques, and most importantly, have fun in the process. Some of the most delicious pizzas come from happy accidents and spontaneous inspiration.

If you've enjoyed this journey, I would love to hear about it! Share your pizza creations, your favorite recipes from the book, or your own inspired variations. Let's celebrate the art of pizza together!

◈ **Follow me on Pinterest for more inspiration:** www.pinterest.com/srmoore536

◈ Have a question, a favorite recipe, or a new pizza idea? I'd love to hear from you! Feel free to email me at **srmoore536@gmail.com**.

◈ Tag your creations with **#PizzaArtistry** so we can see your delicious masterpieces.

Once again, thank you for bringing these recipes to life in your kitchen. I hope this book becomes a trusted companion on your cooking adventures, a source of inspiration, and a reminder that food is meant to be enjoyed, shared, and celebrated.

Now, grab your pizza cutter, take that first bite, and savor the flavors you've created. Your pizza artistry journey is just beginning.

Happy cooking, and may every slice be a masterpiece!

Don't miss out!

Visit the website below and you can sign up to receive emails whenever S.R. Moore publishes a new book. There's no charge and no obligation.

https://books2read.com/r/B-A-XIBBB-LXNPC

BOOKS 2 READ

Connecting independent readers to independent writers.

Did you love *Pizza Artistry: The Canvas of Flavor*? Then you should read *Brews & Bites: A Beer Cheese Revolution*[1] by S.R. Moore!

[2]

"Brews & Bites: A Beer Cheese Revolution" is your passport to a culinary adventure that marries the bold flavors of beer and the creamy allure of cheese. In this tantalizing cookbook, you'll discover the secrets to creating irresistible dishes that will leave your guests craving more.

From creamy beer cheese soups that warm the soul to indulgent beer cheese desserts that conclude your meal with a sweet, savory twist, this book unlocks a world of possibilities in your kitchen. With recipes for appetizers, main courses, side dishes, and desserts, it's your guide to hosting unforgettable gatherings and elevating your home entertaining game.

---

1. https://books2read.com/u/mvBADe

2. https://books2read.com/u/mvBADe

Whether you're a seasoned chef or a novice cook, "Brews & Bites" offers a diverse collection of recipes that span the culinary spectrum. Each recipe is thoughtfully crafted to ensure your success in the kitchen. You'll also find optional variations and substitutions, allowing you to tailor each dish to your personal preferences.

So, if you're a beer enthusiast, a cheese aficionado, or someone who simply loves sharing delectable food with loved ones, "Brews & Bites: A Beer Cheese Revolution" will inspire your culinary adventures. Don your apron, raise your glass, and embark on a flavorful journey that tingles your taste buds and leaves your guests eager for more. Cheers to the Beer Cheese Revolution!

Also by S.R. Moore

Mysteries of Lavender Lane
The Secret of Lavender Lane
The Book Club Conspiracy
The Mosaic Murders

Standalone
Pizza Artistry: The Canvas of Flavor
Brews & Bites: A Beer Cheese Revolution
Souper Fusion: A Globetrotter's Culinary Journey in a Bowl
Slices of Heaven: Sandwiches Redefined for the Modern Foodie
Advent Cookies Around the World: A Global Gastronomic
Journey
Pasta for the Senses
Shamrock & Spoon: Modern Irish Cooking for Every Occasion
Autumn Harvest: Cozy Recipes for Crisp Days
The Autumn Artisan: A Global Exploration of Comfort, Craft, and
Flavor
Love in the Lavender Fields

www.ingramcontent.com/pod-product-compliance
Lightning Source LLC
Chambersburg PA
CBHW060903140726
47996CB00001B/90